LIFE IN LOCKDOWN

John Parsons

Life In Lockdown
© 2020 John Parsons. All rights reserved.

No part of this book may be reproduced in any form or by any means, electronic, mechanical, digital, photocopying or recording, except for the inclusion in a review, without permission in writing from the publisher.

Published by:
Parsons Publishing
Painswick, Gloucestershire, England

ISBN: 978-1-5272-7566-9 – Paperback

Book & cover design by Darlene Swanson
www.van-garde.com

Writing – it kept me busy, it kept me sane and it kept me in touch with my dear grandchildren Lucas and Charlotte

CONTENTS

1. Introduction 1
2. Coronavirus Block Letter 4
3. Coronavirus Block Poem 5
4. Letter Lucas 19/3/20 6
5. Letter Charlotte 19/3/20 9
6. Food Glorious Food Poem 12
7. Letter Charlotte 27/3/20 14
8. Letter Lucas 27/3/20 17
9. Exercise Regime Poem 20
10. Letter Lucas 3/4/20 22
11. Letter Charlotte 3/4/20 25
12. Lockdown Poem 28
13. Letter Charlotte 10/4/20 30
14. Letter Lucas 10/4/20 33
15. Springtime In the Garden Poem 37
16. Story of Thorp Perrow and Douglas 39
17. Letter Lucas 24/4/20 52
18. Letter Charlotte 24/4/20 55

19.	Another Day In Dover Cott Poem.	58
20.	"Daffodils" Letter	61
21.	Haircut Poem	64
22.	School Report Letter	67
23.	School Report	68
24.	Letter May 1st – prelude to Jean Christophe	70
25.	Story of Jean Christophe	72
26.	Letter Charlotte 8/5/20 VE Day	76
27.	Letter Lucas 8/5/20 VE Day	79
28.	Grandma's Going Nuts Poem	82
29.	Learning to Drive Story	85
30.	Brecon Story	95
31.	Why I Became a Teacher	104
32.	Letter Children 29/5/20	116
33.	Letter Children 6/7/20	119
34.	Hotel Disasters Story	121
35.	Letter Children 13/7/20	139
36.	Ode to Juergen Poem	141
37.	Afterword	143

INTRODUCTION

Last year I wrote a book for my grandchildren. It was the record of our family holiday to South Africa, to celebrate my 60th Birthday. Writing it was a source of enormous pleasure for me, and therefore when lockdown was imposed, it provided the ideal opportunity to embark on another project.

This had not been my intention initially. The prospect of being obliged to stay at home had not been announced, but there was huge press and TV coverage of the effects of Coronavirus – in Italy, especially. That country had been put into national quarantine a couple of weeks before such restrictions were initiated here in the UK.

There were lovely stories, despite the circumstances, of residents in apartment blocks across Italy, taking to their balconies and communing with their neighbours, as well as with the outside world, in song. We witnessed wonderful operatic arias wafting across the deserted streets of Naples, Rome, Milan – tutti Italia!

I was delighted by this sense of camaraderie, this joining of communities in uplifting activity, to stir the hearts of a nation and to inspire others around the world. One Saturday morning, lying in bed, listening to the radio, my musings imagined a similar response in this country – more specifically my home City of Liverpool. I pictured a tower block with people singing to each other too – the tune of "Yellow Submarine" came to mind, and my first foray into "recording" lockdown, unbeknownst to me at the time, had begun.

Very soon thereafter, as of 23rd March, we in the U.K. were told to "stay home, protect the NHS, save lives". I love writing letters. I decided that I would embark on the discipline of writing to Lucas (12) and Charlotte (9) each week. It would be impossible to visit them, 200 miles away in York. I do know that there is nothing more pleasurable or more exciting than to receive your very own letter through the letterbox – lockdown or no.

The "Coronavirus Block" poem, sparked other ideas as the days and weeks unfolded. Letters then had to be accompanied by yet another "silly poem". I obliged! As poetic inspiration began to wane, I turned to other possible means of continuing the correspondence. I decided to write episodic reminiscences from my life, as well as initially the "virtual day out" at Thorp Perrow, which we were missing out on. Under normal circumstances, over the Easter holidays, we would have been providing child care, and a day out at Thorp Perrow would most definitely have been on the cards.

Other incidents and memories from my life then became a source of inspiration. I loved teaching, the grandchildren know that – but they did not know why I had chosen to enter the teaching profession. I decided to explain.

Equally, they know how much I love my car and how keen I am to keep it as clean and as tidy as possible. This was the time to give them the reasons.

For those who do not know me personally, it is important that you be aware that I have a slight physical disability. This is congenital, a very mild case of cerebral palsy. No great dramas, but I have a weak right leg and limited function, use or mobility of my right arm. In broad terms this has not affected my career, or my life, but it is relevant, when recounting the story of learning to drive, especially.

What follows is a series of poems and stories, interspersed with snippets of the letters I wrote. These snippets are to frame the passage of time, as lockdown turned from an initial 3 week period of severe restrictions, towards three months of adjusting to a "new normal" – from which we are, as I write, still beginning to emerge.

My thanks to Lucas and Charlotte for allowing me to reproduce the content of personal letters from me to them, during the Spring and early Summer of 2020. I hope that they have enjoyed reading the letters themselves, as well as the accompanying stories and poems. It has provided a real purpose for me, again a source of great pleasure and I hope that you, readers, will recognise some moments from the world we now inhabit, but which none of us could have ever imagined, just six short months ago.

John Parsons
Painswick
July 2020

Painswick

16th March 2020

Dear Lucas and Charlotte,

I am not yet self-isolating, although perhaps someone might now think it advisable to come and lock me up, throw away the key and forget about me.....

Inspired by TV footage of the way in which Italian people have created a community feeling, even in isolation, by going onto their balconies and singing opera, I have imagined such a scenario - possibly Liverpool, but not necessarily. Yeah, ok, it has to be Liverpool.

Scousers, having to stay in, might possibly also decide to sing, to keep "demselves bizzy, toooo beee frenddllyy and toooooo not beee low n lee"

The "song" attached, sung to the tune of "Yellow Submarine" could become the new anthem of the Kop

Walk on - walk on

Lots of love

Grandad x

Grandsad

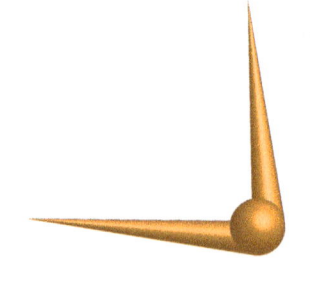

CORONAVIRUS BLOCK

In the town where I am ill
Lots of folk ain't got it still
And they tell us all the tales
Of the things no more on sale
No loo rolls and no hand gel
Nothing more for shops to sell
And they can't go watch the sport
Because there are no games, no more

We all live in coronavirus block
Coronavirus block, coronavirus block
And our friends are all in here
Many more of them can't come near
And the band begins to play
(TRUMPET VOLUNTARY)
All of youse, just stay away….

We all live in coronavirus block,
Coronavirus block, Coronavirus block
As we live our life alone
Order takeaways but just by phone
Shut the door and turn the lock
In our infected block

We all live in coronavirus block
Coronavirus block, coronavirus block

Ad infinitum…..or ad ad nauseam!

Painswick

19th March 2020

Dear Lucas,

When you receive this letter, you will have finished school for the foreseeable future. This is a huge shame, and although the initial reaction of every pupil around the country will be (naturally in a sense!) "brilliant, no school", the reality is going to be rather different, I'm afraid. For you, especially, it will be tough, because I know how much you enjoy every aspect of school life, you have settled in at "Archie's" and are doing really well – recognised by everyone and something you can be really proud of!

Everything is going to be very bizarre for a while. You will discover what plans have been put in place for study via "online resources". I have no idea what that will comprise for Y7, and how that will be managed, monitored....or marked! However it is and whatever it is, I know that you will do everything that is expected of you – and dare I say – hopefully add a little more detail to your writing tasks! You are not one for detail, or for adding info to expand a "story" or explaining a sequence of events, if the bare minimum looks ok!!

I'm sorry that all your clubs have been put on hold too – how frustrating for such an active, sporty kind of guy. I suppose that the trampoline, basketball hoop and "keepie-uppy" will now *come into their own!*

Grandma and I are trying to maintain the discipline of a long walk every day. At the moment we are walking over to Sheepscombe and back round to Painswick – I reckon that it is about 4 miles. I'm writing, to keep my mind busy, something which as you know, I enjoy enormously.

Hopefully you will be able to still go and visit Granny. I know that you and your sister are being very good about ensuring she has company, that you do wash your hands and that she doesn't feel lonely. Equally, I know that you'll be really grown up about every aspect and impact on everyday life, for all of you, as a family. There will be times when you'll be bored, there will be times when you get on each other's nerves and there'll be times when you'll want to shout at everyone. Try to resist that temptation, if you can. I think that mammoth sessions of Monopoly may be in order, as well as many other games that you have downstairs. Also, you have so many books and you enjoy reading so much, that you can set aside "quiet time", not just bedtime, during which you spend an hour (alone perhaps) tucked up in your onesie or snuggled into the duvet, with a great story!

I don't know when we'll get to see you – which again, is a shame, but with Grandma being 162, it is best that I keep her isolated! Seriously, this is a situation that none of us has ever encountered, so we shall just have to see what happens in the coming days, weeks and months. You never know, we may even face time you at some point – scary thought!!

Do take care of yourself, your sister, your Granny and of course your Mum and Dad.

Bizarre times ahead Lukey and I know that you will do your best to help at home, to maintain your brilliant sense of humour and to stay as positive as poss, in the circumstances.

Lots of love

Grandad x

Painswick

19th March 2020

Dear Charlotte,

I hear that you were rather pleased last night, when you discovered that school will finish on Friday! Two more days, as I write and I'm sure that the atmosphere in your classroom today and tomorrow will be a little strange. I imagine that you and all of your friends will be excited at the prospect of not having to go to Lord Deramore's every day and that the thought of being at home – with Erica – will seem very enticing at this stage! (Did I mention Lucas?!!). The thing is Charlotte, I suspect that the "novelty" will wear off pretty soon and that it will be hard for you not to spend time with Frances, Maple, Skyla and all the others in your class.

I wonder what plans Mr. Sharp has, in order to keep in touch and to set you work while everybody has to stay at home. I'm not sure what topics you are doing this term and how he will set tasks "online" – will that be poss? I hear that BBC will have a series of programmes for each year group but I'm not sure how that will work in reality. No doubt there are plans to ensure that you are able to keep up with lessons until everything gets back to normal.

Perhaps you will be like Grandma and do lots of craft – like sewing, knitting and artwork. I hear you've already completed the sloth that we sent you for your Birthday! Have you got any other projects, ready to go? I think you'll have to go to Hobbycaft to stock up – before other families get there!

As you love working on screen and enjoy creating powerpoint presentations, you could do more projects on your favourite animals. Is it still snakes?!! Penguins maybe? Now, I could help you there, after our trip to Antarctica! Did we tell you about the penguin "highways"? These are the tracks that they follow from shore up to their nests and colonies. It really does look like a road full of black and white cars – a single file "lane" going in one direction and an equally well defined track going in the opposite direction! As pedestrians, we had to give way, literally just like at a road junction – and penguin traffic always has priority – no exceptions!

I'm not sure what is happening with riding – both with Katherine and at Nayburn I suspect that they may not be able to continue, which I know will be a he disappointment for you, if that IS the case. I'm sorry about that, as it will be really tough for you to understand at this stage, exactly why such restrictions have to be in place. They do, I'm afraid and no one has any idea yet, just how long all this will continue.

We are fine – as very, very, very (very x 5 for Grandma) old people, everyone tells us that we have to be really careful – we are! I know you are too, when you go and see Granny. I'm sure she loves seeing you and having company – and there is a rumour (is it true, Charlotte?) that you wash your hands to prevent the possibility of spreading germs. Good girl! Wow, after 9 years someone must have told you what that white thing on the edge of the sink in the bathroom is for!!!!

Only joking, you!

When your Mum lived in Australia I used to write to her as regularly as possible – every week if I could, because in those days there was no email, no face time and no apps to enable us to be in touch any other way. As we couldn't go and see her, we missed her and it was a really good way of keeping in touch. Grandma and I will miss not being able to be with you in person for a while, so I shall try to write to you – or send silly songs and poems (did you like "Yellow Submarine"?!). It is something I enjoy and I think you like letters dropping through the letterbox – especially if they're for you.

Take care love, don't get bored, don't be worried and do try and keep everyone happy!

Lots of love,

Grandad x

March 2020

FOOD, GLORIOUS FOOD

Now that we have to stay at home
It's just as well we're not alone,
Do we have some food to cook?
Go to the cupboard…..and take a look.
We've had the lentils and some rice
A big lasagne would be nice……
There's no pasta and no meat
What on earth, what can we eat?
We've got potatoes and some bread
So, chip butties – it is instead!
Fortunately, there's also mayonnaise
Which can be used in many ways
To spread on any kind of meal,
Not Hellman's Light, no only Hellman's Real!

We've got beers and some wine
So Grandma says that we'll be fine!
But, once all of that's been drunk
Then we really shall be sunk
No more food and no more drink
Could get no worse, or so we think…..

So, send food parcels, send'em fast
I don't know how we're going to last…
Sweets, ham pizza and some cheese
And don't forget the Kit-Kats please.

As you know, the fridge is small
We have no freezer, not at all
So we can't store any ready meals
Did I mention we ain't got no Wagon Wheels?

Send food parcels, don't delay
I think we'll barely last a day
It's such an awful sit-u-a-tion
We're on the brink of near star-vat-ion!

If supplies they do run out
There's one thing, I'll think about....
Perhaps, Grandma, I'll have to eat
But actually, there's not much meat!
In fact I think it's only skin
No nourishment, she is so thin!
She's in luck, I'll have to wait
Until she has put on much more weight!
And there's very little chance of that...
Your Grandma, she can't get fat!

So, please send parcels, send'em quick
Tomatoes, yoghurt, that'll do the trick
For six months we can be fed
And please remember what I said
Some pizza, sweets and also fudge,
In anticipation – thank you very much!

Painswick

27th March 2020

Dear Charlotte,

It has been lovely to talk to you on a couple of occasions recently. It really makes us feel, for a few minutes, that we ARE with you in York. I'm so pleased that your collarbone is not giving you any pain or discomfort. I'm sure it isn't preventing your creativity with *Lego*, playing games of cards or reading. Are you able to write yet?

We, like everyone else in the country, are allowed out once a day. When we reach Vicarage Street and walk down towards Dover Cottage, we sometimes see our neighbours. Keeping a safe distance we make sure everyone is fine and chat about the impact on everyday life at the moment. To our delight, a couple of days ago, we saw one of the families opposite. They have a new puppy. She is gorgeous! Not quite as cute as Sam – obviously - but she IS adorable. Her name is Dido, a very small (still – only 11 weeks old) Dachshund. She is black with brown markings – and the loveliest little face! I much prefer her, to next door's cat, which is STILL using our garden as his personal toilet.......I have planted some cocktail sticks – they won't grow, nor will there be any flowers – but they are supposed to stop him walking across empty areas of the border. It hasn't been a great success, I'm afraid.

Last Saturday, we went for a long walk in a village called Sapperton. The village school is TINY and is in fact the very first school where Grandma was Head Teacher. She was only there for one term, from September to Christmas, when the previous Head was away – poorly. It was a lovely time and I have very fond memories of the Christmas performance.

There were only about 45 children in total, in the entire school. Every single child had a part, as they celebrated "Christmas around the World". I remember Grandma sitting on the edge of the stage, surrounded by cowboys, thanking the children and also the parents who had come to watch. It was such a small gathering, she just needed her normal voice.

On our walk, along a canal, we saw a heron, who gracefully took flight as we approached. They are such elegant birds, and as they hover over the water, they look beautifully majestic. I also spied two yellow wagtails. I've never seen them before, but they were lovely too. It was a pair, dancing across the surface of a "pool" of mud, looking for moss, grass and debris for their nest, I assume. There are lots of blackbirds in the garden here too, at the moment. I'm not sure where they are nesting yet, but usually they are behind the clematis next to our shed. I don't think we shall have goldfinch again this year. The nest near the back wall is far too exposed now. I guess that the presence of a cat (have I mentioned him?) won't help either!

As the weather has been so warm and spring-like in the past few days, Grandma and I have been sitting in the garden, enjoying the sunshine. Two days ago, I washed all the garden chairs and the table, cleaning off all the moss, dirt, dust and months and months of muck. I was very pleased at the result. BUT. The very next day, when I went outside, I saw that a bird had already done a poo on the heavy base in which we place the umbrella. Typical! I had to get the scrubbing brush out – again!

I have begun reading a book, which Grandma bought me for my Birthday. (Happy Birthday Grandad! No – finished that now!). It is about North Korea. We went there 4 years ago. So that we can both enjoy it simultaneously, I am reading it aloud to Grandma, as we sit on the patio. It is really good, but Grandma has told me that the entire population of Painswick has joined the "Parsons Book Club". Because my voice is sooooooooooooooo loud, she thinks everyone can hear every word – lucky them, say I!

Now, here's the wonderful thing. When you receive a letter, the most natural course of action, is to send a reply. As I said to your brother, it doesn't have to be *quite* as long as this (700 words or thereabouts), but if you have a mo, in your hectic schedule, then a quick update from Brannanland would be lovely!!!!

A bientôt

Lots of love,

Grandad x

Painswick

27th March 2020

Dear Lucas,

Well, I hope that the Post Office deliver this letter to you more swiftly than last week – this week actually, if we are going to be pedantic! We are counting the number of days that have elapsed since the "stay at home" instructions were issued – it isn't passing very quickly, I have to say.

Enclosed, my latest contribution to poetry, as well as a puzzle from Grandma's newspaper. I tried it a couple of days ago and enjoyed it, so hope you will too. The routines that we have established are now very much the norm – including my writing sessions! I think you'll have to keep everything I send to you, as a form of "archive". In 60 years' time you'll be able to go on the "Antiques Roadshow" and be told by Fiona Bruce that it is a wonderful record of exceptional times, but absolutely worthless! – Alternatively, it may be worth a fortune, you never know!

On our return home a couple of days ago – the young lady who now lives in the house opposite (where Max the Great Dane used to sit in the back of the Volvo), on hearing that Grandma was about to venture to Waitrose, asked if we are vulnerable and offered to go for us! Stifling my laughter (barely!), I said, "yes please". She didn't realise that I was joking, so Grandma had to intervene and explained that our only vulnerability was a lack of beer…..the fact that Louise just didn't "get it" made it even funnier!!

Also, a week or so ago, when people were still working, we walked down Vicarage Street and saw some decorators in one of the little

Life in Lockdown | 17

cottages near the top of the road. The front door was open and they were ripping out everything! There was plasterboard on the pavement, 2 guys were pulling things apart inside, so I said to one chap, "Doing a bit of decorating then?". "Yup" said he," I hope it's the right house!". I roared with laughter and am still chuckling!

Your Mum told me that the schoolwork that has been uploaded for every year group at "Archie's" was really good. I had a quick look and was very impressed by how well everything is laid out for you and the level of detail, to help you cover all the tasks. Naturally, I looked at French et, c'est excellent! Si je peux aider, dis-moi. If I can help, tell me. That said, it was so clear, I'm sure you'll be fine! Moi, j'aime le foot, la natation, mais (but) je suis nul – as you know!!!

When are you and Charlotte offering to make dinner again? I'm told that the pasta was a great success! I didn't look at the Home Economics page on the school www!

Last Sunday we walked across the Beacon, (the den is fine) and then through the valley and home via Sheepscombe. It was a lovely day and there were lots of people out and about. There were picnics, games of football – in fact there were more people up there than when it is snowing. Everyone heads up onto the Beacon to go sledging as soon as there is the merest covering of snow, but I think it was even busier than that, on Sunday. Since then of course, everyone has been asked not to have such gatherings.

Are you able to keep in touch with Matthew, or any other friends, for FIFA or anything else? Is there a "forum" on the Archie's website, to enable Y7 pupils to exchange ideas, ask questions and keep in touch with each other?

It must be really strange and at the same time really great to have everyone altogether at home. It is a weird set of circumstances for you all; I'm sure that you're all enjoying each other's company, having fun at times and helping each other to make the most of the enforced period of "staying put" at number 9!

You are allowed to reply, if you want – I wouldn't mind! Any correspondence doesn't have to be dead long – this letter is about 700 words, so I don't expect *that* number, but perhaps you could manage 100 +!! – ugh!!

On that cheery thought, au revoir et à bientôt, j'espère but I suspect it might be quite a long time – unfortunately.

Lots of love,

Grandad x

March 2020

EXERCISE IN THE TIME OF CORONA

Have I explained my exercise regime?
As I'm a sporty sort – you'll know exactly what I mean
Grandma has said that it'll be really good for me…..
In all honesty, I'd prefer a beer or three!

But no, I'll do a ten mile jog, and then the plank,
At the thought of which, my heart it sank.
I think I'd better start off pretty slow
Because I still ain't pressed the button, "GO".

I've got no stamina, got no puff
In fact a gentle walk is quite enough
But no, it's miles and miles each day
My little legs will soon give way.

Grandma's talking of a fit-bit – or should that be, "bit fit"?
Either way, I'm having none of it!
Exercise – it's all well and good
But let's just get this understood
I'm not that guy who's going for a run
No – that's me – o'er there – sitting in the sun!

I can't really walk *that* far
But as no longer, may I use the car
I suppose I'll have to up the steps
Because next week, comes the real test!

I'll be across the Beacon, round again
Maybe we'll be back by ten
Grandma's made no guarantees
She's not thinking of my knees!

Perhaps, they too, are about to go
I shall have to take it very slow
But no, I can't tell you any lies
I really need this exercise!

Painswick

3rd April 2020

Dear Lucas,

As this is the last day of "school", does it actually feel as if you are breaking up for Easter? It must be really weird! That said, I hear that you've had lots of work to do and that you have been very good and highly disciplined in doing all the tasks asked of you.

Exercise is key – apparently, as we are all subjected to lockdown conditions. Dr. Xand did a programme earlier this week, aimed at adults, in which he talked about the virus, the potential impact on everyone's well-being and ways to ensure that oldies especially, keep a level of fitness, even if "trapped" indoors. He had lots of good ideas and because it was my favouritest medico, I listened attentively. There were lots of suggestions as to how you can manage without any equipment and just make use of the domestic environment, in order to stay in trim. Usually, I "poo-poo" all this stuff, but one in particular made me think, "You know what, I can do that". It was a kind of step exercise, on the stairs, where you move from foot to foot, moving up onto the bottom step and down again – easy peasy! Nope. To Grandma's great amusement, I kept losing my balance, lasted about 20 seconds and thought, "nah". Therefore I shall just have to rely on our daily 4-5 mile trek around the valley, to keep me in peak condition.

A couple of days ago, as were walking along the lane, a police car came towards us. We moved into the hedge to allow him to pass, and gave him a wave. On impulse, I flagged him down, in order to report a serious violation of the new social distancing laws. Pointing at your Grandma, I said, "this lady, whom I don't know, came and snuggled down next to me on my sofa last night. I have 3 very reliable witnesses from York, who happened to be on a video call at the time. They are very reliable and will confirm exactly what I'm saying. They will be ready to testify at her trial, give evidence and ensure justice is served. May I respectfully suggest, Officer, that she be sentenced to 5 years". Being a respectable gentleman of this parish, of course they believed my every word; they arrested Grandma, read her her rights – then they only cautioned her, and immediately released her without charge – ugh. Nearly did it though!!

On another occasion, as we walked home down Vicarage Street, we saw a plastic container full of books, which Ann our neighbour had put on the path behind her car. It was so that people could help themselves, if they so chose. To keep it simple, she had simply written on a piece of paper, attached to the side of the container, "Please Take". Immediately I had an idea, which made me laugh. I explained to Grandma, and she told me off, for being so naughty. The problem was that she too, was laughing at my suggestion. I had asked whether I could move the "Please Take" sign off the container and put it on the car!!! Ann would have seen the funny side (as long as no one ACTUALLY nicked her car!)

Unfortunately, though there has been an unsavoury incident here in Painswick. A few days ago, the village woke up to graffiti daubed over the walls of the Royal Oak pub, opposite the village shop. I was angry, upset and mystified – in equal measure. How could anyone do such a thing? It would be unacceptably awful anywhere but it seems especially inappropriate, unnecessary and horrible in a quiet, peaceful place like Painswick.

Life in Lockdown

A stealth bomber flew right over our house too. It was really low – we had seen one before, in Cirencester, near an air base where they are stationed occasionally. I think it was rather overkill to have that fly over, to make sure that we were all staying at home!!

Grandma told you on the phone about the new trampoline that Poppy has in her garden. It IS ginormous! I think it is actually even bigger than the Big Top for Gifford's Circus! It has a wide "high-vis yellow" stripe around the rim of the netting – not sure why, but it was perhaps that which prompted the fly-past!

I noticed that your hair is still really neat, really smart and dead trendy. What am I going to do for 6 months? I'm already beginning to look a little dishevelled and unkempt – no idea what I will look like by the time I'm allowed to go to the hairdresser. One thought: I shall borrow Grandma's "Alice Band", brush it all back, put a bowl round my ears and shave off everything below the band. I shall then look exactly like Jack Grealish – no bad thing – what do you think?!!

Have a lovely weekend, enjoy your "school hols" and do come into shot occasionally, when we are talking to your Mum and to Charlotte!

Lots of love,

Painswick

3rd April 2020

Dear Charlotte,

Many thanks for your card! I'm sure that the guinea pigs will love being outside, once their "run" is in place. You told us that you had drawn a plan of where it would be placed in the garden, but didn't explain exactly which position it will occupy. I'm guessing in front of the kitchen window, leading up to your nature study, so that you can watch from both ends of the garden, and it leaves the other side free for football – am I correct?

Yesterday afternoon, I was able to plant some sweet peas in the garden. I had sent away for them, as the garden centres are all closed. It is a little early, so I have to hope that there is no overnight frost, or that will kill them – if the cat doesn't! Early, in the sense that I normally plant them in May, and they grow up the "obelisk" near the patio and provide a profusion of beautifully bright, sweet-smelling flowers throughout the summer. Do you remember our picking them almost every day, to go into a little posy on the kitchen windowsill? I also gave "Cousin It" a haircut. He's the plant, in a pot by the steps on the patio. He looks a little sorry for himself, especially as I have had to put a tall cane right in the middle of the pot. "Why?", I hear you ask.....well, someone, and naming no names (no, it wasn't Grandma!) had sat on it, flattened all his hair and done a poo. Yuk. To prevent my feline foe from repeating that horrible trick, the cane will stop him, unless he wants to end up looking like a pussy cat lollipop on a stick!!!

We are still going for a long walk every day. We venture out towards Sheepscombe, or over to Edge (where you and Lucas had an enormous Sundae last summer). We have been really lucky to see lots of wildlife. Two young deer darted across a field, right in front of us at the bottom of Vicarage Street, which was so lucky. Their little white bob tails were flicking from side to side. It reminded me of the white ring around the bottom of waterbuck in S Africa. I wonder if there is a springtime surge in animal activity or whether they feel emboldened because there is so little traffic, no noise and barely any people around.

The alpaca and the ponies are still happily munching in their field. In the meadow opposite there are 2 lovely Shetland ponies. As we approached, the other day, they both trotted to the wire, to say "hello", or so I thought. One did stay, nuzzling, wanting a carrot or a lump of sugar, but the other took fright at the sound of my voice. He looked at me disdainfully, promptly turned round and yes – you've guessed it – did a poo……something of a pattern here! We saw a girl riding her lovely pony around the perimeter of a huge field and then later on another girl, perhaps a little older than you, sitting on her pony, at the entrance of a large house (far enough away to be safe); she was chatting to an old gentleman, standing on the doorstep. I imagined that it was her Grandad.

I imagine that you think today is the last day of "school", as officially, before the lockdown, this would have been the last day before the Easter Holidays. Nope. I have a lovely, brilliant, wonderful surprise for you – honestly! I've been in touch with Mr. Sharp (mrsharp@learnmoreY4Deramore.con) and we have come up with the following plan. As he misses all of you soooo much, he is going to visit each pupil in his class for half an hour, to check on all your work, your progress and your tables (seven sevens = 77!). We decided it would be easiest to do it in alphabetical order, so because you are a "B", you will be amongst the first to receive a visit – lucky girl!!

Do you have lots of rainbow drawings in the windows of houses nearby? There are quite a few in Painswick. There is a large one pinned to the gate of Yew Tree House, the big one next door but one, as you go up our street. It was done by Iris. Iris is in Reception at the school here. She often sits on our little wall on her way home. Everyone knows her. She has s had a tracheostomy and therefore has a tube in her throat, to make sure she can breathe properly. We often chat to her Mum, who told us that Iris had cried, when she was told that she couldn't go to school "for a while". Apparently she burst into tears and said, "but Mummy, I have to learn my spellings". I wonder if there was a similar reaction from you and Lucas!! What do you mean, "not a chance!".

Take care, keep calling us from time to time, before you go to bed, we love hearing from you and seeing you, as we can't actually be with you in person.

Lots of love,

Grandad x

LOCKDOWN

We always watch on in dismay
To see what's on the news each day
The way in which the disease evolves
And how this problem can be solved.

We're told that things will get better
That's what it said, in Boris's letter
Did you receive a copy too?
I'm sure that it did also reach you
We must frequently wash our hands
A message, everyone now under-stands
That includes you ma chére Charlotte
Cos you don't really – not a lot!

We must keep up levels of hygiene
To ensure hands and face do stay clean
This way we can avoid infection
Such is the pro-fess-ional suggestion
To stop the spread in different ways
Like stay indoors for days and days
In fact it might be weeks – or more
We just can't say, cos ne'er before
Have we faced such a situation
That affects us all across the nation
Stay at home and don't go out
That's what this is all about.

On our daily, permitted walk
We simply step from our front door

Instantly onto the Cotswold Way
Head off in any, any way
Whate'er we want, any sugg-estion
We set off in any dir-ection
North or South, East or West
Over the top, to Edge, is best!

It affords such lovely views
Across the fields, past lambs and ewes
Buzzards soaring high up in the sky
We always hear birdsong nearby
Squirrels, rabbits, even deer
So quiet it is, they sometimes dare come near.

As Spring, abundant, blooms and grows
All her beauty, Nature shows – in bushes and hedgerows
In Sheepscombe, Slad and in Wick Street
So few people do we ever meet
In this glorious countryside,
It lifts our spirits, optimism revived.
In these calm valleys concealed
The beasts and birds are now revealed
Rabbits running, swallows darting overhead,
We have witnessed an entire season unfold
A story, a fable that just had to be told!

Painswick

10th April 2020

Dear Charlotte,

The card you made for Easter is beautiful. The decorations on the outside are lovely, and the Easter eggs, heart and star inside were a wonderful surprise – thank you! I shan't eat the sweets until Sunday, Easter Day, as that was the rule when I was growing up. It would be like opening a Selection Box in advance of December 25th!

The weather here is glorious and our daily walk has allowed us to see some wonderful scenes of nature. The other day we noticed that there were some new-born lambs in a field. One, to make sure it stayed warm, wasn't snuggled up next to his Mum, but was sitting on her back! I've never seen that before. The lovely, woolly bed was obviously very comforting for the little chap. Yesterday, I saw two swallows darting across the sky, just ahead of us. They come back to the UK for summer, having been to the warmth of Africa for the winter. There is a saying, "one swallow doesn't make a summer", but as I saw two, it MUST mean that the cold of winter has now disappeared – until November, hopefully. One of the big houses on our walk round the valley from Sheepscombe had a notice on the gate. It said, "If the gates are open, please do come and enjoy our garden. Please do maintain social distancing. Enjoy". What a lovely invitation! We did not go in, but from the lane, looking over the wall we could see a carpet of crocus and anemone across the entire lawn, bordered by waves of daffodil and tulip. It looked brilliant. How kind to allow people in, especially at the moment.

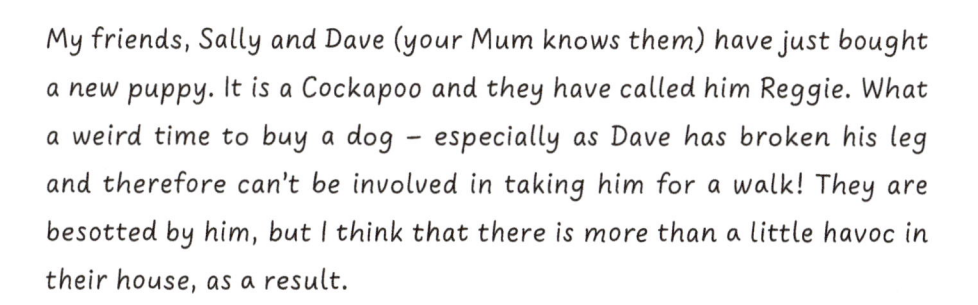

My friends, Sally and Dave (your Mum knows them) have just bought a new puppy. It is a Cockapoo and they have called him Reggie. What a weird time to buy a dog – especially as Dave has broken his leg and therefore can't be involved in taking him for a walk! They are besotted by him, but I think that there is more than a little havoc in their house, as a result.

Sally says:

> Well ….so far Reggie seems to be settling in really well. We had two frightful nights to begin with, he cried all night long, it was worse than having a baby but we persevered and stuck it out without going down to comfort him and the last couple of nights have been fine apart from a few whimpers on waking. He goes to bed at nine and wakes up at five and then he comes bounding up to our bed for snuggles & yes I did say we would never let him upstairs !! His personality is developing and I can see he's going to be very confident and good natured, he is already well-behaved, eager to please, quick to learn and to be honest there's been very little mess really. He goes outside for poops & wees and so far no accidents, apart from one little poop on the kitchen floor. It's early days though, he's still finding his feet & If it all sounds too good to be true, It probably is !

Dave says:

> Reggie is chewing everything, but at least is going through the night without barking!

I just can't imagine how disruptive it is for them!

I told you about Iris, in my last letter. A couple of nights ago, when we were having dinner, we were aware of something happening outside, on Vicarage Street. When we looked up, standing on our driveway and waving happily at us, was Iris. She was wearing a face mask, and obviously very pleased to see us. We couldn't go out and chat, probably just as well, because she really does have to be careful not to be exposed to any infection.

Did you hear about the supposed instruction from the Government, that all cat owners had to ensure that their pets were kept indoors, during the lockdown? I was thrilled because I thought that it would mean an end to the daily "poo patrol" (not Paw Patrol – that *would* be allowed!). My euphoria was short-lived, because the very next day, there was clarification from the British Veterinary Association, saying that cats are allowed out after all. Ugh. My "feline foe" from next door, celebrated, in the only way he knows how......he had dug a hole really close to my newly planted sweet peas, so I wasn't "peased" or should that be "pleased"!!

Have a lovely Easter! It will probably be "had" by the time you read this, because there are no collections or deliveries over the Bank Holiday.

Very glad to hear that your collarbone is on the mend and that it isn't stopping you from being active, until you can get back on your bike and also your horse!

A bientôt –

Lots of love,

Grandad x

Painswick

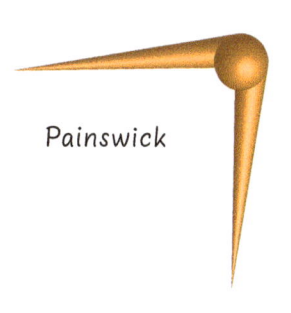

10th April 2020

Dear Lucas,

Thanks for your letter and also for the sweets – brilliant surprise! You mentioned "fishfingers" – how did you know? Grandma managed to buy the very last packet of the large ones from Waitrose. (You know, the big jobbies you always have when you come here in August). They are for tea tonight, as I've been such a good boy. Not sure what Grandma's going to have, though! No, we haven't fallen out yet – cheeky young man! – as noted above I had sufficient incentive to behave myself (well, this week at least!) and Grandma, rather like someone else I know from this family, keeps saying, "I have been good, haven't I?!!"

I appreciate that I AM very old and am perhaps confused, or perhaps have "got the wrong end of the stick", but can I ask, why have you got a "Nine to ten Light Switch"? *There is a light switch in your bedroom, every room in your house, if I remember correctly and it just seems a very expensive treat, when you have electricity everywhere, already. Is it that it's an automated, magic light switch, which allows you to read in bed, between 9 and 10, without your Mum and Dad knowing? Does it switch on, as soon as it hears them go downstairs and then switches itself off at 10, to alert you that it is time for sleep? Or, am I missing something?!!!!

Life in Painswick is even more peaceful than ever. There are very few people about, and with the exception of tractors and the odd delivery van, very little activity. That said, the community is working very hard to make sure that everyone is fine. You might be aware that there are lots of really old people who live in this village (go on, say it, I know – that's why we're here!), who are on their own and who can't necessarily get out, to do their shopping, for example. At the beginning of April, when the village magazine was delivered, inside was a card. It was printed on both sides. On one side, it is green all over, with the following message in white letters, "No help required, thank you". On the reverse, on a red background, it says, "Self-isolating, in need of help" and then a white box, in which you can write your telephone number. This can then be displayed in the window of your house, so that people can see that you are in need of assistance. Isn't that a wonderful idea? I was so impressed, because it will reassure the old folk especially, that they won't be all alone, should they fall ill.

We are still doing our daily walks through the valleys around Painswick. It doesn't sound as exciting as all of your outings. You've obviously been able to find new pathways, new routes and lots of different tracks around the University, Heslington – and beyond. Given the strict restrictions on movement, I do feel obliged to alert N Yorks Police that you are flouting the rules, by having a family walk AS WELL AS a run – how naughty!!!!! No, it's great that, despite the lockdown you are all keeping active, having lots of exercise and getting lots of fresh air! That said, I think you had better take care on yon trampoline – I hear they can be vicious beasties and can attack at any moment – leaving facial injuries as their customary "calling card"! Careful, as your ultra-cautious Grandad, I am just looking out for your safety – I suggest your cycle helmet and your swimming goggles in future!!

Last weekend, quite coincidentally, on Saturday and Sunday, we passed two families, out for a walk. Both had little boys (5 or 6 years old) wearing LFC kit. As everyone always greets each other, from the opposite side of the road, of course, I congratulated the kids on their choice of team and said that we had deffo won the league this year – whatever happens or is decided by the Premiership. One smiled shyly, the other looked utterly miserable. Hid Dad explained that he'd just fallen off his scooter (how do you fall off a scooter?!) and had scraped his knee. Quick as a flash, I said, "Mo Salah wouldn't let that stop him". Dad replied, "that's his favourite player". It seemed to have the desired effect because the little boy (almost) smiled!

I'm glad that Premier League players, led by Jordan Henderson, have begun a fund, to contribute money to the NHS. I had imagined that it would have happened weeks ago. Mo Salah, for example, has paid for a village school for his home in Egypt as well as other contributions to the community he grew up in. As you know from the biography you have, he had a very tough childhood. I would have thought that he, or indeed any other really rich footballer would have "started the ball rolling" (pardon the pun) and donated money, or made a gesture of support in some way. Something is happening now, so better late than never!

Have a great Easter and enjoy playing with your light sabre – no sorry light switch

Lots of love,

Grandad x

*Nintendo Switch (so I'm told!)

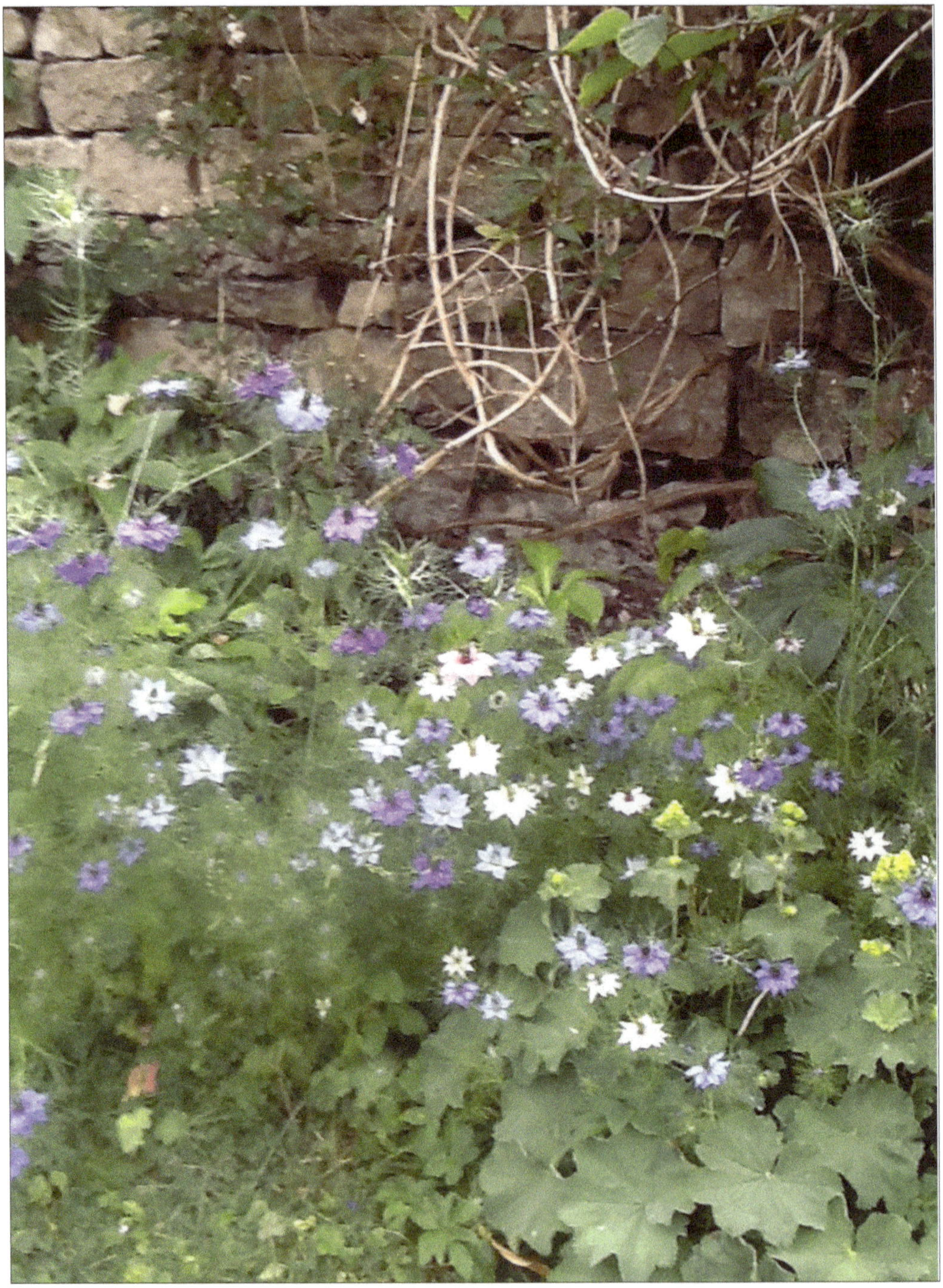

April 2020

SPRINGTIME IN THE GARDEN

After months and months of rain
At last, the sun's come out again
Spring, at last, has now arrived
And once again, we can be outside.
Eating, reading – on the patio
It's a little sun-trap, as you know.

There's some colour, as the plants come out
That's what my garden's all about.

Last Autumn I bought a lovely rose
Let's see what happens – no one knows……
I found it for a shady spot
To brighten up that bottom plot
Dig in deep, the instructions said,
Up till now, it isn't dead!
I planted it with care, as I was told
And the winter was not especially cold,
So I hope that it will thrive,
Or at the very least, survive!

With me, it's really trial and error
And of course, some sunny weather!

At the moment we have some daffodils
Beautifully swaying, even still
Lots and lots of flowers here,

Though not as many as Grasmere,
Where Wordsworth "wandered as a cloud"
Not now we can't, we're not allowed!

So in the garden, we must stay
There's lots of things to do all day
In flower too are the hellebore ……..
(not moi the bore)
And this year, there are even more
They have spread – all self-seeded
No help from me, as none was needed!

Bluebells soon will al-so appear
That surge of growth is really near.
Buds are showing on our pear tree
Could be a bumper crop – let's see!
And of course, "love in a mist"
Loads of this – there always is,
Aided by your spreading seeds
Every year it even outgrows weeds!
The foxgloves too are looking strong
They'll shoot up, before too long.
That will attract all of the bees
It's truly lovely, when one sees
Their hovering in and round each "bell"
It's the way that we can tell
Summer's here – and all is well!

THORP PERROW AND THE STORY OF DOUGLAS THE MEERKAT

Whenever we spend time in York, we enjoy days out in lots of different places. Over the years one of our firm favourites has been Thorp Perrow. It is a wonderful destination, just outside Bedale in North Yorkshire. It is primarily an arboretum and throughout the changing seasons, it has beautiful displays of flowers, ever-changing vistas and wonderful displays of trees.

My favourite time of year to visit, is Hallowe'en. The autumnal colours are magical. There is a burst of yellow, orange and the deepest reds you have ever seen, when the foliage on the Maple trees, Acers and others are providing the most wonderful display of riotous colour as they begin to shed their leaves. On a crisp, dry autumn afternoon, it is a brilliant place to play in those fallen leaves – it does have to be dry though! Lucas and Charlotte take great delight in having "fights", gathering fistfuls of brown, papery foliage, which is then strewn across the lawns – occasionally landing a shower of tree on each other's head. Equally, it is tremendous fun, to gather the leaves into one huge pile and then dive headlong into the mound!

On one occasion this was witnessed by two much younger children. One could see the excitement – and anticipation – cross their features, as they watched the two older children squeal with delight. They so desperately wanted to join in! However, their Mummy and Daddy seemed to be reluctant – perhaps they would get dirty, perhaps they might hurt themselves, perhaps it was not quite seemly to have youngsters jumping into piles of fallen leaves. The children beseeched their parents. They relented, but Grandma and I could tell that they were still nervous and quite apprehensive at what accident might befall their darling off-spring. Without being asked, Lucas and Charlotte stood back to allow the little ones to have a go – they loved it! As the pile of leaves became more scattered, all the children began rebuilding the mound, for maximum fun! As they dived, they whooped with delight and we could see the adults melt, as they realised how much enjoyment was being derived from such a simple pleasure. As we had had enough, we bade them farewell, smiling and watching as these two now uninhibited toddlers dived, again and again into a mass of leaves. Even as we were disappearing out of view, we could still hear their voices shrill with laughter. The loveliest thing was that by this point, the parents had relaxed totally and were helping rebuild the pile and encouraging their much-cherished darlings to be even more daring in their play!

During every school holiday, there is always an activity trail, organised for children. Easter Egg Hunts, Santa – but the best and the scariest, is the Hallowe'en trail. It is so well organised, so well laid-out and the "props" are fantastic! There are sound effects, witches hovering overhead, huge tarantulas lurking amongst the branches, skeletons waiting at bus-stops – barbecues set up with body parts, eyeballs, fingers and thumbs on the grill – so many awfully, awesome displays. We always have great fun, following the pathways, finding clues, solving the puzzle – and ultimately winning a prize!

Life in Lockdown | 41

At first, it was as if we were the only people who knew about this wonderful place. We would arrive, at lunchtime, and head immediately to the picnic tables near the stream, just before the arboretum "proper" starts. Of course, we would always sit in the same place. Lunch would be: sandwiches, ham or ham and tomato for Grandad and Lucas, Charlotte cream cheese and cucumber and Grandma whatever was left over!! We would have Hula Hoops – plain for Charlotte, Salt and Vinegar for Grandad and Cheese and Onion for Lucas and for Grandma. The children also had a fruit "yoyo". We'd then have an apple, followed by – and this is where the adventure and unpredictability comes in – either a Wagon Wheel or some "jammie dodgers". Call me old-fashioned, but this final element was all just a little too much. It reminds me of the TV ad that ran in the 1980s when schoolkids are queuing up for their school dinner and sing, "Will it be chips or peas?". Well, substitute "Wagon Wheel" and "jammie – dodger" and judge for yourselves, the sheer level of excitement, during our days out!

When we have finished our lunch, we always then go to the Adventure Playground. There are swings, a zipwire as well as a fort constructed across two trees. There are lots of walkways, secret paths and then a slide to come down, to reach the ground again. Sometimes it can be really busy nowadays, so Lucas and Charlotte like to go and hide and play in the trees and the woods which surround the Play Area. Grandma and I sit on a bench, strategically placed on the perimeter. The children's mission, is to sneak up on us – unobserved – possibly from any direction. As spies, they are very careful not to be spotted, diving between open spaces, hiding behind crates which are dotted around or concealing themselves in or around the fort. Inevitably, they manage to surprise us and it is a very rare occurrence that we manage to see their approach or their eventual pounce, from behind the bench.

After a while, we have to head off, through the gardens, but not the swamp garden at this stage. We have to reach the display area where there will be birds flying, at 1.30. We always make sure that we are there a little before the start, so that we can grab a seat near the front, with a great view. If we have time, we walk around the compound, saying "hello" to Colin, George and Mildred as well as many of the other birds of prey, housed in different sections of a lovely aviary. The display always starts on time, with George and Mildred. This is a pair of caracara. They are really excited to be out of their enclosure and run around – in huge anticipation, because they know that they are about to have their lunch. They must work for it though! Small pieces of food have been placed until containers on the grass, before they are taken out of their aviary. They can very easily upturn the containers to retrieve the morsel of meat underneath. The person looking after them then puts pieces in a huge bin and they jump in, and emerge, triumphant, with the meat. Fascinatingly, they don't eat it immediately. Instead, they store every piece, in their crop – for later. This is to replicate their natural instinct, which would be vital, for survival in the wild. They gather as much food as possible, while it is safe, so that they can eat it later, without fear of any other bird, or creature disturbing them. The crop is like a large yellow shopping bag, under their chin. The more they "consume", the more noticeable the bag, as it fills up with everything they have swallowed. Apparently, caracara are particularly attracted by the colour red. To prove this, the keeper erects a small "washing-line" with 5 pieces of material pegged on the line. Without fail, every time, the birds go to the washing line and peck the red piece of material onto the ground. How does a bird manage to do that? Everyone always laughs; George and Mildred seem to know that it is the "finale" to their performance and are then happy to be "cajoled" back to their enclosure.

Colin is then brought out, for his turn. He is a Turkmen Eagle Owl; he is most certainly our favourite. He has beautiful piercing eyes and we know exactly when he is watching us! He is always impatient to be taken out of his aviary, for the same reason as the caracara – food! One can almost feel the disdain that Colin feels, being obliged to "sing for his supper", or in his case, fly for his lunch! There are 4 posts, one at each corner of the paddock, which is the display area, He trundles across the ground, swaying from side to side, before he, seemingly reluctantly, jumps on to the top of the nearest post to him. The keeper then coos to him, tempts him with a tasty morsel, to fly over the heads of the gathered spectators onto another post. This "game" holds not one jot of spontaneity for Colin, but he knows that if he is to be rewarded with some food, then he jolly well just has to get on with it – and comply. This sequence continues for several "fly pasts" much to the delight of the enraptured audience – Colin, less so!

There have been 2 occasions on which things have gone terribly wrong. Firstly, at some point, Colin (obviously not as daft as he looks), spied a field mouse on the path at the rear of the paddock. Here was a "free lunch". He was off like a shot, speared his prey and proceeded to tuck in – thank you very much! No amount of cooing or protestations from the keeper would entice him away from his tasty snack – we were transfixed, amused and delighted to see this subversive reaction, to an opportunity for "fresh food"!

The second occasion on which things were far from perfect, in terms of a display, involved Grandma. Not wanting to steal the limelight, she decided that Grandad should have a starring role too……Colin, as described above, was "going through the motions" of entertaining the crowd, by flying overhead. This time though, he thought to himself, "I know. I'll give them all a shock, a bit of a fright, I'll come in really low!". Which is what he did. Ever so low, that he almost clipped Grandma's head. She was perched on the bar (like a bench but with no back). As Colin approached, possibly to sweep her into his talons and have *her* for lunch, Grandma instinctively ducked, lost her balance and fell backwards, spiralling towards a bumpy landing. In an attempt to break her fall and to stop herself, she grabbed hold of me and pulled me backwards. We both fell in a heap, no harm done, other than to cause huge embarrassment – but huge amusement to all the other on-lookers!

On another occasion, I was watching the display, when I felt something on my head. I assumed that it was a fly and ran my fingers through my hair. Immediately, I felt a piercing jab on the back of my hand. I realised that I had been stung by a wasp! It was really painful but I was very brave! I didn't want Lucas and Charlotte to notice, or to think that their Grandad was a wuss! That said, I was thinking to myself, "I hope it doesn't swell up too much, or become too painful, thus preventing my driving everybody home". Fortunately I was fine and very, very brave (did I mention that?), so was able to get us all safely back to York. What a hero, Grandad!

Lucas, who witnessed this scene, was delighted, to such an extent that he bought a "cuddly toy" Turkmen Eagle Owl at the shop. I shall give you one guess as to the name he gave his new "pet", which had almost carried off his beloved Grandma, to a fate worse than death! Yes – of course – he is Colin and is now a beloved member of the family. He has been to "Cub camp", football tournaments in Blackpool, holidays in Gloucestershire and Salcombe. In fact the only place he hasn't been is Turkmenistan – home! That said, we did offer to take him with us, when we visited that country last year!

The final part of the display is always a falcon. We have watched the saker falcon many times. The bird, as with the others, is flown with the prospect of a meal at the end. This is done by the falconer enticing the bird to fly, to soar across the sky and then to dive down, plunging from a great height, swooping across the field. The lure is twisted away, out of range and the bird flies off again. It then does a circuit, in full view, if you can concentrate sufficiently well, before once again targeting the lure in his eyes and heading towards the field. You can hear his approach, because there is a little bell attached to his "collar". To ensure he has enough exercise, and to replicate conditions in the wild, this circling, swooping and not being allowed to claim his prey is repeated several times. Finally, at a given vocal signal from the falconer, the saker flies in and is allowed to take the lure. Immediately it is in his jaws, he runs off, creates a mantle around his prey and then is left, undisturbed to enjoy his lunchtime reward. The "mantle" is when the bird opens his wings and "wraps" them around the mouse or vole, to protect it from view and the possibility of another bird trying to steal the meal! The word "mantle" as in "mantlepiece" over a fire, has the same origin, in that the "mantle" protects an open fire.

Once, when the display was over, Lucy, one of the falconers came out with Douglas. He was a young meerkat, on a lead. He had been "rejected" by the troupe and had been "adopted" by Lucy. We were able to go and stroke him. Lucy told us that meerkats can live to be 10 years old. He was so cute!

After that, we always walk through the rest of the animal area, to see meerkat island and to feed the wallabies in their enclosure. We buy special food for both species at the little shop (where we also adopted Colin). Nowadays we don't actually purchase meerkat food. You have to throw it towards the island, and chickens who patrol the footpaths always manage to grab the food first! We are all happy to see the chickens – with one notable exception. As soon as we leave the shop and walk across the garden towards meerkat island, the chickens immediately see their best friend, Lucas. He doesn't feel quite the same way! Despite this, every chicken runs towards him, just him, to greet their "bezzie mate", to ask for some meerkat food or simply say "hi", as they have obviously missed him soooo much since our last visit. Lucas runs, zig-zags across the garden to avoid them, tells them to say hello to Charlotte, or Grandma maybe, but they just won't listen! It is dead funny to watch! I digress. We therefore don't feed the meerkats any more, but head straight to see the wallabies. Very often, in the summer especially, they are resting in the shade beneath the pine trees. Sometimes though, they are hopping around the field and will then approach the pathway, especially if they know you have some food for them – which we always do. You can crouch down, they will come and take the pellets from your hand and allow you to stroke them, which is lovely! A few of the wallabies have a joey in their pouch. They are a little more shy and won't approach you, but they are quite close, so you can see the baby, nestling in the warmth and comfort of his pouch.

Once we have finished there, we always walk back to the café, via the lakes and the tree-lined avenues. We pass through the "bog garden", which as you can imagine, needs no further explanation! It is a lovely stroll and in autumn we always stop for the obligatory leaf fight – as long as it is dry!

When we reach the café, Grandad finds a spot, hopefully on the terrace and Grandma goes to buy coffee, juice and cakes – "rocky road", if at all possible. We then meander back to the car, via one last visit to the adventure playground, if it isn't too busy and then drive home. We always have a lovely day out at Thorp Perrow and this story is to remind us of what always happens when we visit. This year it isn't possible, so this "virtual tour" is to remind us what we have missed!

I mentioned Douglas the meerkat. There is a story about him. As I explained, he was "rejected" by the troupe. He was probably the runt of the litter and wasn't strong enough. Therefore Lucy "adopted" him, fed him at her house, bought him a little bed and trained him, so that he went to the loo in her garden. To ensure he could always get out, she had a cat flap (meerkat flap!) made for the kitchen door. When he was old enough-and sufficiently strong, she bought a lead for him.

This enabled her to take him for walks and then to meet people at the end of the falconry display, which I explained to you earlier. This worked really well. Douglas loved Lucy, Lucy loved Douglas and they loved going for walks and meeting all the visitors to Thorp Perrow. He liked it when visitors asked lots of questions, and was very reassured to hear that he would live until he was 10 – how old is that! He was so glad that Charlotte has asked that question! He was so happy that he allowed her to stroke him for ages – far longer than anybody else that day!

On one occasion, when Lucy needed to go and pass a message to the lady in the shop, she walked through the wallaby enclosure and then on, past meerkat island. Douglas was really interested and said hello to the wallabies – he had never been that way before, and then suddenly got a whiff of a strange smell…..strange, but at the same time very familiar – but he didn't know why. Then, out of the corner of his eye, his right eye, he caught sight of someone who looked very similar to him. He knew it wasn't a mirror image, Lucy had a mirror in her lounge and she had held him up, cradled in her arms, so that they could look at themselves. So that wasn't the answer. Then there were others, running across the sand, a few were rushing underground, into burrows, wow that looked exciting and there was one, standing on his hind legs, on the top of a mound. He was obviously on guard.

At the same moment that Douglas gazed at that meerkat – he realised they were all meerkats – the guard stared right back at Douglas. He began to shout to all the others. He screamed, "guys, there's a meerkat over there!". His head was twirling around and he was trying to make sure he didn't lose sight of the poor prisoner, being dragged away, to what fate, what horrible torture, he wondered. "I think he's been kidnapped!. That lady has got him in chains. There is a tight collar around his neck, a choking harness across his back and she is dragging him away – where to? Where is she taking him?". All the other meerkats on meerkat island, as that was where Lucy was walking with Douglas, ran around, excitedly, looking towards Douglas, all feeling really sorry for him. There was nothing they could do. There were still visitors in the park, it was broad daylight and they couldn't leave the island, or everyone would know *their* secret.....

"Keep watching! Don't let him out of your sight" they shouted to the guard. Lucy disappeared into the shop. "We've lost him", one shouted. Fortunately, after a few minutes, the lady reappeared – and was still forcing the meerkat in chains, to follow her. "There they are", shouted the guard. He was so excited, he jumped down and started running around. Another meerkat took his place on the look-out mound – and continued to watch as Lucy approached the island again. The meerkats all watched in silence this time. Once they had gone by, the new guard was told, by his younger brother, "keep watching. See where they go. Don't let them out of your sight!". Phil, the meerkat atop the mound was straining to keep the lady in view. He was jumping up into the air, to make sure he could see exactly where she was taking the ensnared meerkat. "I can see the roof, I can see the roof of the cottage! She must have taken him in there – maybe there's a dungeon".

"What's a dungeon?", asked one of the pups, who was watching from the safety of the entrance to a burrow. "It's like a burrow" explained Phil, "but there's no escape, there's no second entrance at the other side, it is made out of stone, so you can't get out – ever".

"We need to try and rescue him", said James – a cousin. They all belonged to one big, extended family and James was always in the thick of all their chasing games, which were great fun. "I know. We'll go and try to rescue him, tonight, when it gets dark. Me, Phil obviously and then we'll need 4 others, to make sure we can cover ourselves, have look-outs and encircle the house. Right, I want Simon, he's dead brave, you Colin, John too and finally Nick – agreed?"

The six meerkats were ready to leave at 7 o'clock. They couldn't go before that, because the keeper brought their dinner at 6.30 after all the visitors had gone home for the day. Colin always had to have dinner and they all decided that they needed food, to keep them going – it was going to be a long night……

"But they all live on meerkat island", I hear you say. "So, how on earth can they leave their home and go on a rescue mission"? Well, now I can reveal their secret…..they can – and regularly do – leave the island, after the keepers have left, at the end of each day. The chickens, who always eat their food, are in fact very good friends to the meerkats and they carry them across the moat; nobody has ever seen that happen, because they are so careful. Normally, it is to allow all the animals to play together, when nobody is watching. No one knows! They join the goats, the chickens, the wallabies and they run around the grounds, playing hide-and-seek, "tag" and having relay races. The wallabies usually win!

Tonight though, is different….rather than avoid the house, where Lucy lives, they gather in a huddle, to confirm their plan. Phil will go first, the others will follow, Colin will be look-out and Simon will take up the rear, to make sure they aren't followed, or seen, from the other side of Thorp Perrow.

As they approach the house, which has lights on in the kitchen, they can hear a voice. "Lie down, Douglas", it says. She must be about to torture him! They must hurry, to help him, to save him. But how? When they reach the back door, they have a huge stroke of luck. There is an opening in the door, that they will be able to go through. It is a kind of flap – a cat flap or in this case, a "meerkat flap"! The lights go off and there is silence. "She's plunged everything into darkness, to frighten him even more. He'll be terrified. We must hurry" said John. There was no sound. Total silence. "She must've gone to get the ropes to stretch him. That's why he had to lie down" said Phil. "We have to go, now, before she comes back and it's too late".

Very bravely, he stepped forward, leant against the flap and pushed as hard as he could. At the final moment, he fell through and landed, in a heap, on the kitchen floor! Douglas, who was just dozing off to sleep, sat bolt upright in his basket and whispered, "who's there? What's happening?". He thought it was a cat, a strange cat, and was rather frightened. Then, he sniffed and caught that strange and yet familiar scent that he had noticed earlier that afternoon. "Who IS IT?" he said, more loudly and a little more bravely. "Phil. My name's Phil and we've come to rescue you, before you're tortured and thrown into the dungeon, forever".

"Who is "we"?" asked Douglas. So Phil explained that he, his 2 brothers and 3 cousins had mounted a rescue operation, because they had seen him being led away in chains by the lady, earlier that day.

Douglas didn't understand. "But I'm not a prisoner", he explained. "I live here with Lucy. I have my own bed, and the meerkat flap is to allow me to come and go as I please, into the garden for our cottage". Then he realised. They thought that his lead, which was to help him stay by Lucy's side was "the chains" that held him captive! He continued, "I live here, because when I was little, I was very poorly and Lucy didn't think that I would survive on the island. I was too timid and too tiny to get my fair share of food, so she decided to bring me home and look after me. We go for walks and I meet lots of visitors every day. I didn't know where the meerkat island was, until today. We never usually go that way, so I just thought that the cottage was my only home".

"You, Douglas – but you are our kid brother" said Nick, who by this time had joined Phil in the kitchen. "I remember, our litter was 4 pups, me, Phil, Colin and …and you! But you disappeared one day. Mum tried to look after us all, but as you were so tiny, it was really hard. We missed you, we didn't know where you had gone. All the time you were so close by – you're safe – that's brilliant".

"My brothers?", gasped Douglas. "But I don't remember at all."

"You were too tiny" replied Phil. "But now we've found you again. I can't believe it". He then had an idea. "Listen, every night, when Thorp Perrow is closed, and the keepers have gone home, we all get together and play all over the grounds. We have races with the wallabies, we play "tag" and "hide-and-seek" can last for ages because there are sooooooooooooo many places to hide. Why don't you join us?"

"Wow! Can I?" Douglas was beside himself with excitement. "I'd love that" he shouted with glee.

"SSSHHHH", said Phil. "Lucy will hear you".

"Sorry", said Douglas, "but I can't wait". He was wide awake now and jumped out of his basket and followed the others outside, through the meerkat flap.

That was the start of a regular night time playtime, that none of the keepers, not even Lucy, nor any of the visitors to Thorp Perrow ever knew about.

Lucky Douglas to have met up with all his family again.

THE END

Painswick

24th April 2020

Dear Lucas,

It was very good to see you the other night, perched precariously on the end of your sister's bed! It sounds as if the new "term" is providing you with a lot more work. I'm sure you are already much more used to "remote learning", finding data, programmes, platforms and uploading everything into the appropriate file – at the right time. It sounded really complicated at first, but I think by now you'll be a "dab hand"! Although it isn't ideal – I know you'd much prefer to be on site at Archie's, it is a really good way for you to become accustomed to independent research and learning. It is such a wonderfully useful skill, especially for later on, in 6th Form or University – and indeed for your chosen career, whatever that will be....

I hear that you've had some problematoes with your teeth – you are your Grandma's grandson – the question is, did the tooth fairy visit, twice?, or is she in lockdown too and therefore not able to do the necessary financial transaction?!

I told Charlotte that we walked past the Edgemoor pub, and saw the landlord in the garden. As we have known him "for ever", we stopped and had a chat – at a safe distance. I asked if there was any beer left, or had it gone back to the brewery. The beer there, which I like, is called "Bob". I always ask for a pint, mimicking the voice of Rowan Atkinson in "Blackadder". (ask your Dad to do it for you – I know he CAN!). The gentleman explained that he'd had to pour 3 barrels of the stuff down the drain – quelle horreur! I remonstrated and said, "you could have called me", at which he laughed! A great shame, to

52 | Life in Lockdown

waste such amber nectar. He told me that the brewery wouldn't come and collect it, from Bristol, as it just wasn't cost-effective.

The lady who now lives in the house opposite us, where Max the Great Dane used to sit outside, has been poorly. She thinks that she has had the virus, because her temperature has been high, she's been really tired and not feeling right. A few days ago, she felt a little brighter and decided she would sit in the sun for a while. She was obviously a little worried still about being ill, so I uttered reassuring words, told her she looked fine, and that it must just be a mild dose of Coronavirus, the warmth and the sunlight would be beneficial, etc etc etc. She brightened a little, sounded "reassured" and asked if I had a "medical background"! No, I explained, I just talk a good game, or words to that effect! Well, until that moment, I had managed to make her feel a little better!!

During our "Listen with Grandad" sessions, when I read aloud to Grandma, we had a book by an author, Laurie Lee, who lived in the next valley, in a village called Slad. It was a series of reminiscences from his childhood, in the 1920s and 30s. It talks of days out in Painswick, going to school, playing with friends as well as stories about the history of the area and weird characters who lived hereabouts, at that time. We found it fascinating, because so much of the geography is familiar to us, nothing much has changed in that regard and you can really imagine the scenes he describes. He explained that Wick Street, a hamlet between here and Stroud, actually refers to Painswick. It was, hundreds of years ago, the main "road" or track at the top of the valley (parallel to the main road that we drive down towards Stroud). It was used for moving livestock from location to location and just shows how long there have been farmers working in this area. It was

Life in Lockdown | 53

extremely evocative and when we next did the walk along that road, we were looking out for all the things he described, from 100 years ago. Some we did, like the milestones, some of the old cottages and "big farmhouses" – fascinating!

I hope you get respite from schoolwork over the weekend and that you all have a restful (ha!) time!

Lots of love,

Grandad x

Painswick

24th April 2020

Dear Charlotte,

It was lovely to talk to you a couple of nights ago, although it was well past your bedtime – no wonder Daddy came in and put the lights off! It sounds as if you are all being extremely active, staying very busy and taking lots of exercise. I'm glad that your arm is properly better now. Although we have all been in "lockdown" for over a month now, somehow it seems even longer since you fell off your bike. I bet it does for you, too!

We have a very relaxed routine – nothing like as frenetic as yours – but we do enjoy our long walk every day. I have worked out that I have walked well over 100 miles, since we started having to "stay home". That means that I could have walked over half the distance to your house. Another couple of weeks and I could "pop in" for a coffee, before heading back to Painswick! Well, not pop in, I suppose; I would have to wait outside, while you opened the front door, left a mug on the step and then retreated indoors again. It would be lovely to see you "in real life" though!

In the past few days, we have seen so many different things – yesterday, we disturbed some deer, who were in a wooded area next to the road. Grandma spotted them first, but then they darted off, prancing really quickly, jumping amid the trees. It is always so wonderful to see them. I also saw a pair of goldfinch (no, not goldfish, they can't fly!) – they are really small, but have a distinctive black head, with a little red "cap" right at the top. That's how you can spot them, even though they are so tiny.

Life in Lockdown | 55

We saw a family in their garden, blowing up a large paddling pool – not with explosives, but with a pump! It is so warm, that they decided it would be wonderful to have a splashing time! As we walked past the Edgemoor pub, (where you had that HUGE sundae), the landlord and his wife were in the garden. I asked if he could make us a sandwich, but unfortunately that wasn't possible!

A couple of nights ago, when Grandma and I were having dinner at the dining table, I became aware of something, out of the corner of my eye. It was Iris (I've told you about her already); she was sitting on the wall. As I turned round, she pulled tongues at me – huh! So I pulled tongues back and pretended to cry. We both burst out laughing at the same moment! She was on her way home with her Mummy. I think that they had been putting up another "poster". "What posters, Grandad?", I hear you ask! Well, all the way up – and down – Vicarage Street, there are now pictures from stories, including "Stickman" and "Gruffalo". Each picture is in a protective see-through "wallet", and there is a typed "rhyme", which is something to do with "staying at home". One of the Gruffalo pictures, shows G following mouse through the forest – but at 2 metre distance, to stay safe! All of them are fantastic and because it is Iris and her Mummy who have done them, everyone thinks it is wonderful.

The alpacas and the ponies are getting to know us, I think….the ponies especially will often come to the edge of the field (not the one in the opposite field, who did a poo when he saw me). We can't feed them, or even stroke them, but it is lovely that they come up close. The alpacas are enjoying munching their way through the new leaves on the bushes around the perimeter of the paddock. They stand, extending their necks, just like giraffe, in order to reach up as high as they can – weird. Tell me, Mrs. Vet-to-be – are alpacas from the same family as giraffe? If not, then I think they should be!! On one occasion, as I entered the lane, at the bottom of the field, I ducked to avoid a branch and as I did, a huge wood pigeon flew right out, almost knocking in to me – I'm not sure which of us was more shocked!!

Have a lovely weekend – not thinking about "rivers".

See you on screen, soon, I hope!

Lots of love,

Grandad x

March 2020

ANOTHER DAY AT DOVER COTT

Another day at Dover Cott.
What have you done? Frankly, not a lot….
Read the papers, had a walk
We come home and then we talk
And begin to reminisce
About the things we now do miss.
Of course there is the "aminal game"
But it really isn't quite the same
When guessing, it is just we two
It ain't quite right, without the two of you!

We've done some washing, all our clothes
But we won't be needing much of those
Onesie, jim-jams, knicks and socks
Is all you need to watch the box!
As you lie and watch the telly
Who cares if your tee shirt's smelly?!
But really it's important, to take care,
Brush your teeth and comb your hair
Basically, you must look your best
Don't open the door in knicks and vest!

Another day at Dover Cott.
One thing I so very near-ly for-got
It is vital to keep to your routine
You'll understand exactly what I mean.

58 | Life in Lockdown

It really helps to pass the time,
First, we get up, between half 8 and 9.
I'm up first and have break-fast
Just how long, can a cup of coffee last?
Grandma has a shower – does her pil-a-tes
Does that for half an hour, most days.
She stays upstairs for exercises
I stay down here – yes – that's the wisest!
Because I'm not a sporty sort
I suppose, perhaps now, I really ought
Try to do some lunges, press-ups too.
I'll send proof, on video, to you
That should give you all a laugh…
Worry not, I'm not THAT daft!
Actually, literally, I sit, I read, I write
Check all my messages from overnight
Write replies – and po-ems compose
And perhaps once this virus goes
A volume shall be published of my verse
There's not that much, that could be worse!

Another day at Dover Cott.
Am I bored? Ab-sol-u-tely not!
I can check the garden, plant some flowers
Then I can play for hours and hours….
Weeding here and pruning there….
There's just one thing that makes me swear….
And that is next door's ruddy cat
But do not get me going, not on that.
You'd be pretty angry too
If, every day, you had to pick up poo

I've tried all sorts, to scare it away
But he always finds another spot
I think the damned thing should be shot!

Another day at Dover Cott.
Counting the days….my, there are a lot.
For weeks maybe, we'll be isolated
And the only thing that leaves us devastated
Is the fact that you aren't here
But we know you can't come near
Cos we are old, so very old
And therefore must do, as we are told.
You must therefore stay away
See you! We both long for *that* day!

Painswick

April 2020

Dear Lucas and Charlotte,

This week marks the 250th Anniversary of the poet, William Wordsworth. He lived in the Lake District and wrote many poems about the fells, the countryside and the beauty he witnessed in that rural "idyll".

One of his most famous poems is called "Daffodils". The words are hugely evocative of a scene he witnessed on a spring day on the shore of Ullswater. Everyone assumes it is Grasmere or Rydal Water, where he lived, but it is no less beautiful, whichever location it refers to.

When I was 7, in 1966, I remember visiting Dove Cottage, (no not Dover Cottage, that's somewhere else!), the house where he lived. It cost sixpence (6d) which is the equivalent of two and a half p nowadays. I remember it vividly. My Mum and Dad allowed me to go in on my own, a huge deal (!) and there were little rooms, containing books, manuscripts and lots of very dark furniture. It obviously had a huge impact on me, because I have never forgotten that day.

A couple of years later, when I was in what is now Y5, I had to learn "Daffodils" for homework. In those days, every Monday we had to learn a poem and then recite it out loud, if selected from memory. I was always disappointed, if I wasn't chosen! That was not the end of it though! We then had to write it out – perfectly – all the spelling correct, all the punctuation, apostrophes, everything. As I have (or rather, had!) a good memory, this was the perfect test for a child like me. Miss Deakin, my really fierce, elderly English teacher was really

Life in Lockdown | 61

scary. Even though I was "good" at English, she didn't like me (the feeling was mutual). The written test was always marked out of 20. If I didn't get 19 at the very least, I was very disappointed — as was my Dad! Fortunately, as I enjoyed the task, it was rare that I got into trouble for not achieving a good mark.

Miss Deakin, despite being so frightening, was a good teacher and it is she who taught me to love words, writing, reading and of course grammar and punctuation. She was a demon and a real "stickler" for accuracy! She was a good friend of Miss Barrow. She too was very old, or so it seemed to me, as a little boy. Neither was married; they came from the generation when women were obliged to stop teaching, if they ever got married. Miss Barrow was quite the opposite — she was kind, warm, encouraging and she liked me, and my Mummy!! As a family, we used to go on holiday to the Lakes. We stayed in a family-run hotel near Ambleside. It was delightful, and I have very fond memories of it. Then, on one, memorable, nay totally unforgettable half-term break, we walked into the lounge of the hotel. I was transfixed by utter horror and total fear. Sitting in the comfy chairs by the window were two very familiar figures — none other than Miss Barrow AND MISS DEAKIN — Aaaaagggghhhhh! Miss Barrow was welcoming, warm and genuinely pleased to see the Parsons family. On the other hand, Miss Deakin was, I think, even more shocked than I was! She could barely speak and when she did address me, she called me "Parsons"! In those days, at that school, we were called by our surname. How awful — on every count. I suppose it must have been pretty dreadful for them too. Just think teachers on holiday, a break from school and a kid you teach walks in...... imagine if Mr. Sharp appeared at Robin Hood's Bay!!

We managed to avoid them mostly, although evenings after dinner, in the lounge were TORTURE! I shall never forget. That said, neither have I forgotten everything that the fierce old woman taught me. Miss Barrow is someone I remember fondly. She was the Head of the Prep School. I was there, when I was away from school for another operation in Alder Hey Hospital (of "Operation Ouch" fame) and she was very kind when I came back to school. She arranged for one boy, who became a good friend, to tie my laces for me, when we put our shoes on, in time to go home. That was after "prep class" (homework club). We used to sit on the floor in her study, learning our spellings (I loved that too!).

That is today's story, I shall keep them coming, if I can remember them!

Lots of love,

Grandad x

May 2020

HAIRCUT

You know things just aren't very fair
Today, a lady should've cut my hair
She always keeps it nice and short
Just as well – and so she ought
Because there's really not much left
And if I go bald, I'll be bereft!

Perhaps, then, I'd transplant my beard
Now, that would be pre-tty weird!
I hope that it won't get that far…
I'll find a potion – in a jar
That I rub in and leave to soak
Then I shan't resemble a decrepit bloke!
If not, then I'll just have to wait
And hope, beyond expectation, it's not too late,
In 6 months' time to get it cut
Perhaps even sooner – with any luck!

If it grows, it will go curly
So very long, so very "girlie"
I don't think that I shall mind at all,
But Grandma will "go up the wall"

She hates it, when my hair is long,
Have to say, she isn't wrong!
But as it's really thinning out
I think there's really little doubt

That by the time we see you next
My lovely locks will pass my neck…
Either that, or all will disappear
And all you'll see is head and ears!

That prospect is not a great look
As in the mirror, I shan't even dare to look
The follicles will produce no hair

Life in Lockdown | 65

And my bonce will all be bare!
Maybe you won't recognise the handsome chap
With nothing, nothing on his scalp....
And you, if you ever dare
Can say, "Grandad, where's your hair?"
The only thing on top will be a shiny tan
What a gorgeous looking man!

In Liverpool, for hair, they say, "hur"
You know it rhymes exactly, just like fur
Perhaps I could get a squirrel for my head
Just make sure, it's really dead
It'll keep my brain cells warm,
The coolest thing I've ever worn!

Painswick

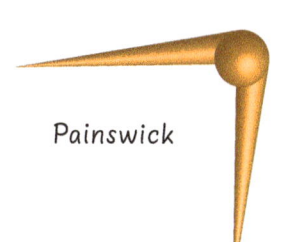

4th May 2020

Dear Lucas and Charlotte,

When I was rooting around (ratching as Great Grandma would say!) for the photos from France, I came across some other stuff, from a long time ago!

The School Report is from the end of my first year – in David House – the Prep School for Liverpool College. The form list from Christmas 1966, was saved by my Father. It shows my position in the form after that term, a mixture of the work during the term and the exams. Yes – we had exams every term! Don't be like Grandma, who scanned the list, from the bottom upwards and said, "I can't see you anywhere!" – cheek!

There were 24 boys in the class – at half-term that summer I was second overall! I also had 2 "impositions". That was the name for a punishment. You had to stay in and write lines....I don't know how I had been "naughty" but no doubt it involved talking, when I shouldn't!

```
                    XMAS 1966

            FORM 1.
            Mrs. M.E. Lindsey
        Woolven M.W.
        Edwards R.D.
        Langford A.C.R.
        Tapp D.L.N.
    5.  Parsons W.J.
        Weir A.M.
        Melrose J.
        Tuson J.J.F.
        Richardson M.D.
    10. Clements B.G.
        Berman J.M.
        Kitchen P.J.
        Ball M.P.
        Cocker J.J.
    15. Bezley J.R.
        Blackmon M.H.O.
        Dean N.R.P.
        Hughes N.S.
        Rhodes R.D.
    20. Collins T.J.
        Spiers A.G.
        Pritchard J.D.
        Williams S.T.
        Crowther R.J.
```

Life in Lockdown | 67

I was only 7 when I started there. It says "Form 1". There was also "Lower 1" and "Upper 1" – 6, 7, or 8 years old, when you started. I had to sit an "Entrance Exam" in February 1966 – just before my 7th Birthday. It was Maths, English and General Knowledge. Maths was ok – I had learnt my tables, I had practised long division, adding, taking away, multiplication....English I liked and could write a story as well as complete the Reading Comprehension exercise.

	Marks%	Place		
DIVINITY			Good work and sound progress.	
ENGLISH	91	4	From time to time there is a real improvement in his handwriting. He does not find this subject difficult; so he can afford to work a little more slowly for the sake of legibility.	
HISTORY	70	6	He has done much good work this term and he contributes a great deal to discussion lessons.	
GEOGRAPHY	70	8		
ARITHMETIC	84	2	He takes new work in his stride and he is able to correct his mistakes. He is making an effort to use mathematical instruments, in spite of difficulties.	
NATURE STUDY			Very good. He is working more quietly and sensibly.	
HANDWORK AND ART			Good. He has worked with determination this term.	
MUSIC			Only fair. Much more effort needed still, to develop and train his aural sense.	

Name: Parsons W.J. Form: 1 Age: 8:4
No. in Form: 24 Calling-over Position: 7 Half-Term Position: 2 Average Age: 8:5
Summer Term, 1967

Days absent: — Times late: — Number of Impositions: 2
A friendly boy who is steady in both work and behaviour and is making good all-round progress.

General Knowledge though was more difficult. As you are studying "rivers" Charlotte, you will appreciate this story. One question read: "Which river runs through Liverpool?". Well everybody knows that it is the Mersey – as in "Merseyside" as well as the song, "Ferry across the Meeersssseeey". However, at 6, I didn't know that. My mind was

68 | Life in Lockdown

searching for the right answer, but I just couldn't retrieve the info – simply because it wasn't there. I therefore wrote, "the North Sea". Sea was a bit of a give away – that ain't a river, but I was satisfied it wasn't a bad "guess". Well, when I told my parents about THAT question – they never let me forget my particularly dumb answer for many, many years!! Fortunately, I passed and was therefore allowed to start in September 1966. Miss Barrow was the Head Teacher (I told you about her elsewhere), and she was very kind. The horrors of Miss Deakin were still to be revealed, in following years!

I had to write today, so as the saying goes, "May the Fourth be with you!"

Lots of love,

Grandad x

Painswick

1st May 2020

Dear Lucas and Charlotte,

May already! This means that we have been imprisoned in Painswick for more than a month – somehow it seems much longer! I wonder how long Boris will keep us under lock and key – will we ever be allowed out again? By the time restrictions are lifted for all age groups, apart from the very old (70+) Grandma will have reached that landmark Birthday and will not be allowed out of the house!!

The story enclosed, has many happy memories. I loved working on "colonie de vacances", but it was really hard work – almost like being Mum AND Dad to 6 or 8 children for a month – yikes! In 1979 I did 2 months – July, then without any break, other than the coach ride back to Paris, to collect the next group, all of August – by the end of the summer I was exhausted. I went home to my parents' house for a few weeks, before going back to university. For the first week I was home, I slept most of the time and they let me, which was very kind! I would wake up late, haver breakfast, read, have lunch, doze for most of the afternoon, have dinner and then early to bed. Gosh, I can actually remember how physically drained I was – but it was worth it!

The weather has been horrible this week. Even as I write this letter, the hail stones are dancing onto the window and no doubt wreaking havoc in the garden – ugh! It will not stop us venturing outdoors though, for our daily trek across the valley. Yesterday, despite wearing several layers of waterproof clothing, we were soaked by the time we arrived home. En route we saw a fox, who ran out in front of us, along a little lane, trotted ahead of us for a little while before darting into the undergrowth, through a gap in the hedge.

A couple of days ago, as we were walking past a field with cows in it, a calf caught sight of us and ran across to the perimeter fence. I suspect he thought we were the farmer (and the farmer's wife!) with some food for his lunch. All of a sudden, every other calf as well as the bigger cows also saw us and rushed over, just in case they were missing out on something exciting. Each animal had a 6 digit number on a tag attached to their left ear. I explained to them all that I didn't have any food for them. I spoke to one, number 106372, but it didn't sound as friendly as talking to "Daisy" or "Flossie". Some had a tag on their right ear too – one had 23-5-18 on it. I presume that was her Birthday! Under the date was written "SILVER". I couldn't decide if that was her name, other than 106493, or whether she had won silver prize and come second in the "Best Cow in Gloucestershire" at the County Show! I shall never know.......

I trust there have been no (self-inflicted) injuries on the slackline and that the competitive spirit has not led to daft challenges, bets or daredevil stunts by either of you or your aged parents – no more A & E please! Cycling is far safer (well, up to a point, I suppose, Charlotte!).

Lots of love,

Grandad x

THE STORY OF JEAN-CHRISTOPHE

When I was a student, during the summer holidays I was able to go and work in France. This was a brilliant way of immersing myself in the language, being in the sunshine and being paid. It wasn't very much money at that stage, but that wasn't the most important element for me – I just wanted to be in France.

I had become involved with an organisation which trained young people, so that they were ready to work with children. I had also been on a course in northern France, which was also designed to prepare you for such a role – a "moniteur" or "monitor" on holiday camps – "colonies de vacances". Because I had completed these courses, I was on a list of candidates to work in these "colonies".

Schools in France normally have 8 weeks of summer holiday, so children are not in school for the whole of July and also all of August! Because this is a very long time, very often companies would arrange camps, so that the children of their employees could go on camp – usually for a month at a time. Children as young as 6 are sent away, to the seaside mostly – and don't see their parents for 4 weeks. They are looked after by volunteers, "moniteurs", sleep in dormitories and spend much of their time playing on the beach – which can be great fun.

Luckily, I was offered a job on a camp run by part of the French Government – the Ministry of Finance. We call that "the Treasury" in England. As they had a lot of money – obviously – and really did want to look after the children as well as possible, the camps were very well organised, with nice facilities and good food.

I had to arrive at the Ministry early one morning, at the beginning of the school holidays. After a while, I was introduced to the director of my camp. He and his wife and their 2 children, Nicolas and Laure (9 and 6) were getting everyone organised. There was a coach ready for us, and eventually after taking the register, we were able to set off.

I had a dormitory of 8 boys, aged 8 – and we had a wonderful summer. I learnt so much French! As children have a more limited vocabulary than adults and the topics of conversation are normally all to do with "day to day" activities and routines, I was able to pick up lots of expressions and ways of talking, that just don't appear in text books – so from that point of view it was brilliant.

As it had gone so well, I decided to sign up again the following year. I was able to work with the Ministry of Finance again, which was great. I knew the routine, knew the director, some of the other volunteers and really enjoyed looking after the children. This second year, I had a mixed dormitory – 4 little boys and 4 little girls – aged only 6. It was a real shock for some of them! Once the excitement had died down, often they would become upset, as they missed their Mummy and Daddy. I remember especially, Katherine, Dorothée and Jean-Christophe. Katherine didn't want to be looked after by a man, Dorothée clung to me at every opportunity, but the one I recall most is Jean-Christophe. He was a cheerful boy, happy and because his elder brother and sister – Yves 9, and Béatrice 8, were also in the same camp, he never felt homesick or lonely.

However, most nights, usually at about 3 o'clock in the morning, I would be woken up by him, climbing on to my bed and saying, "John j'ai fait pipi dans mon lit" – John, I have done a wee in my bed…So as not to wake all the other children, I would remove his jim-jams, dry him as best I could, and then put him back to bed, at the foot of the bed, where the sheets were still dry. I would reassure him that we'd sort it out in the morning. We always did – but he kept the laundry very busy! He wasn't being naughty, nor was he drinking too much, or looking for attention. There was a very understandable reason for his behaviour – he was scared, he was traumatised and he had nightmares, during which he wet himself.

Why?

At the age of 3, at home in the kitchen, he had pulled a pan of boiling water from the stove. It had fallen across his neck, his chest and the top of his left arm. Fortunately not his face. He therefore had terrible injuries, and scar tissue over much of his upper body. He had had skin grafts, but at such a young age the area of burns was large, seemingly still livid and very unsightly – poor kid. He was terrified of water – several times a day he would say, "John je prends pas la douche" John, I'm not having a shower. The water showering onto his head would remind him of the accident. Therefore, every evening, I had to bathe him in the wash basin. You know the photo, Charlotte, of your Mum washing you in the sink, when you were a baby? Well, it was rather like that! We had a laugh, it got him a it clean, but I made really sure never to swirl water around his face and never attempted to wash his hair – that didn't matter.

Yves and Béatrice were really kind, Every day, they would come and check that their little brother was fine, that I was fine (bless!) and that he wasn't scared. Yves had been told by his Mummy to look after Jean-Christophe; he took this responsibility really seriously. Béatrice was a wonderful big sister, and was always giving him hugs and kisses. Because they were older, they were not in the same dormitory.

We would go to the beach every day – group by group, so I always had my eight little ones with me. Dorothée always wanted to hold my hand, my left hand and very often Jean-Christophe would be hanging onto my right arm. One day, he beat Dorothée to it and was holding my left hand. Dorothée indignantly strode over and said, "Moi, je prends la main gauche" – Me! I take his left hand. To which I replied, "well, take my right hand". Her response, as quick as a flash, was "I don't like that one". "Nor do I Dorothée, but it's the only one today", said I. She tried, to her credit, but couldn't hang on to my right arm as well as Jean-Christophe had become accustomed to doing!

As we walked down the beach one day, Jean – Christophe stopped dead in his tracks. He was staring at someone sitting on the beach. I followed his gaze and saw a gentleman, who was obviously on his holidays – but he had had his right arm amputated. Jean-Christophe could not take his eyes off this man. Fortunately he was sitting with his back to us, and therefore did not witness this little boy staring so blatantly at him. Jean-Christophe looked at the man, looked at me and then looked down at his arm. He said, "that man has only got one arm". "Yes", I replied, "and we've got two, aren't we lucky". He thought for a second, as this sank in, said, "yes" and then ran off to catch up with the rest of the group. He obviously had never seen, or indeed ever imagined anyone losing an entire limb – and realised that despite the scars, he was a lucky boy to have 2 arms.

I never understood why, but even at 6, he could barely write. Every week, each child would write a post card home (before email, face-time or mobiles!). Of course it was very limited, and I did much of the work. All of them could at least manage, "Bisoux" and their name. Not Jean-Christophe. He couldn't even begin to spell his name! Had he been called "Jo", perhaps it would have been easier! I therefore decided to make it my mission to teach him how to spell his own name. We had very little time, but there was a period of siesta every afternoon, after lunch. So, for a few minutes each day, I would help him, to try and write his name. Copy, yes, up to a point, but retain it until the next day – nope. Gradually, we made progress and finally, finally, for the very last post-card, I wrote something to his Mummy and Daddy. I then called him over, read it to him and asked if he would write his name at the end. He did! What a clever boy! I was really proud of him. When I spoke to his parents, I explained that he had written his name, all by himself, and his Mum was really pleased.

Later in the year, I received a letter from Marseille, where they lived. It was a lovely "thank you" note from his Mum. I still have that letter and sometimes wonder what ever became of that brave little boy. Nowadays he will be a little younger than your Daddy and a little older than your Mummy.

Painswick

8th May 2020

Dear Charlotte,

As today is a Bank Holiday, I'm not sure exactly when this letter will reach you, as there are no collections from post boxes – sorry. The Holiday is to celebrate VE Day, the end of WW2 in Europe. It is a moment when I think of my Mummy and Daddy, as both of them served, during the war. Mum was in the WRNS – Women's Royal Naval Service. She was stationed under (yes, literally under, in the tunnels and rooms beneath) Dover Castle. She helped to monitor the movement of ships in the English Channel. This was to ensure British vessels were safe from attack. When she was there, at one point Churchill visited – so important was the work that she and the other Wrens (that's what they're known as) were doing. My Dad was still in Germany on this day, 75 years ago. He had helped to liberate a concentration camp and then after that, continued towards Hamburg. He was part of the forces which entered that City and set it free from the Nazis, in April 1945. I always think of Mum and Dad on occasions such as this, because I know that it would have held huge significance for both of them.

It is now 7 weeks since lockdown began. We have watched Spring emerge, gradually and now spurt really quickly, as everything bursts into colour and is growing so rapidly. In that respect, I have enjoyed witnessing, every day and every week, the emergence of new growth. On one beautiful old house nearby, the ivy wasn't even in bud at the outset – now the beautiful fresh green foliage covers the entire wall at the side of the property.

We walk every day, as you know. I have now calculated that I have covered the distance between Painswick and Nursery Gardens! In fact by now, I reckon that I could be in "Piglets"!! I could have the bouncy pillow to myself – just like you and Lucas used to wait until there were not many other children, if any, before you played on it! You were "social distancing" even before we all have to!!

We missed all the excitement of a police chase through Painswick, in the early hours of Sunday morning. There were 5 cars chasing a stolen vehicle, driven by drug dealers, apparently. They obviously thought they could take a short cut through the village and shake off the police who were in pursuit – but they drove down Vicarage Street and then turned into White Horse Lane, which is a dead-end. (the little hill we walk down when we come home from the Rec, down the steps). The abandoned the car and ran away, down past our house and into the valley beyond. Even though a helicopter, with huge searchlights circled above, trying to find the villains, they managed to get away. There was lots of noise, blue lights, sirens – Grandma and I slept through everything! All of our neighbours were amazed that we didn't hear a thing – but we did not know about our very own episode of "Traffic Cops" until they told us about it.

Iris tried to come and see us a few days ago….she was at the top of the steps and we, and her Mummy, had to stop her coming down into the garden. She was asking lots of questions and wondered where the door, by the garden tap, goes – so I told her it was a magic door! She is still putting up pictures around the village, which are on walls, gates, in front of people's houses – it always puts a smile on everyone's face. We even found a new one yesterday!

I stood and watched a squirrel the other day. He was sitting on top of the "outhouse", next to a neighbour's front door. He was not at all concerned by my presence – but when he'd had enough, he ran along the top and then disappeared into Ann's garden. I've also seen my first wren this year as well as coal tits, whose head is almost totally black – hence the name, I suppose!

I hope that your project on rivers is going well and that you are doing lots of other "school-related" exercises, while your brother is doing his hours and hours of work every day. It is really kind of you to help out with some of his subjects – what a lovely sister you are!

Looking forward to seeing you again soon, on your Mum's phone.

Lots of love,

Grandad x

Painswick

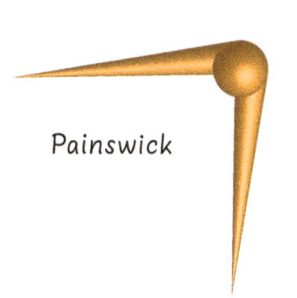

8th May 2020

Dear Lucas,

All the celebrations to mark VE Day are cancelled today, for obvious reasons, but it does not diminish the significance of the day, nor the commemorations for the end of the war. I find it particularly poignant, as I think of my parents. Both saw service – Dad would be 96 this month, Mum 95, if they were still alive. Like many of their generation, they never really spoke about their wartime experiences, but I do know that it left a lasting mark on each of them.

My Dad will have witnessed awful scenes of cruelty and the ravages on prisoners as he was part of the liberating forces of Bergen Belsen, a concentration camp in northern Germany. From there he went on towards Hamburg, which was also liberated. Many years ago, I found an archive of photos and documents relating to this, in the crypt of a church in Hamburg. I spent a couple of hours, looking at everything, willing myself to see my Dad. Of course I didn't, but seeing young British soldiers in the main square, any of whom *could* have been him, was very moving. It gave me a real sense of those days. My Dad would have been the same age as I was, when I was looking after Jean-Christophe in France. A totally different world, all possible because of the sacrifices of those who served in WW2. Hamburg is nowadays totally rebuilt, of course and a place I love. I even went there to watch a quarter final match during World Cup 2006 – Italy v Ukraine – 2-0 to Italy! It was a brilliant atmosphere in the stadium as well as in all the pubs and bars across the entire City.

I have walked well over 100 miles since Grandma initiated my regime

Life in Lockdown | 79

of daily route marches through the Gloucestershire countryside! At the start I was 5 foot 10, but my legs have worn down so much, that I am now barely 5 foot 8! I know this for sure, because the heel on my walking shoes has worn down so much, on the left foot. I need you to contact the RSPCG (Royal Society for the Protection of Cruelty to Grandads) and report her. It shouldn't be allowed, in the 21st century!

We walked past the Edgemoor pub again (sundae special). The landlord has put traffic cones at the entrance to his car park as well as a huge breeze block. This is to prevent drivers parking there, while they go for a walk. I sat down on the breeze block. He asked. "What are you doing?", so I explained that I was forming a queue, so that I'd be first in, once he was allowed to open again. "I think you'll be waiting a while!" came the reply! Still waitin'.....

I have been converted to the cashless society. Until now, coins and bank notes have been fine. However, in the village shop, I have "gone contactless". Wow, what a wonderful idea! Well it is, until you realise just how easy it becomes, to spend money! I thought that during lockdown I'd barely spent anything – no lunches or days out, no petrol for the car, no treats, no new blue shirts, no shorts for the good weather, no nuttin – I can save for a Nintendo GS (Grandad Style!) – no I can't. I had a bank statement through the post. I opened it, safe in the knowledge that I'd be loaded with dosh, for the reasons I have just explained. But then I saw multiple "entries" – transactions – for "Best One" (the shop) – and nearly died! Do you know how much, exactly how much I have spent there since the end of March? No, you don't, but I am about to tell you. Now, imagine, it is only newspapers, beer, stamps and Eccles Cakes (the odd pint of milk for Grandma) – I added it all up, without a calculator mind, so it was a very big sum (in both senses of the word) – and do you know that the princely sum (again) was a grand total, no not a grand total, a hugely, gigantic, enormously, humungously incredible total of one hundred and fifty six pounds and 55p!! £156.55 – I reckon the biggest amount must be on stamps! I told you first class postage was exxy – I didn't appreciate just how much it must be (still don't know though!) to write to you and your sister every week!!

As Eccles Cakes and beer are essentials (unlike milk and papers), I suppose that I just have to accept this drain on my finances!!

I hope that Dad managed to cut your hair beautifully and that the fringe is now out of your eyes, so that it doesn't flop into your face, thus preventing your seeing the screen, and completing your daily dose of school work! I have to say, I am *very* impressed to hear how much time and effort you are devoting to your remote classroom – well done you!

Have a lovely weekend – but not sure exactly which weekend, by the time you read this letter!

Lots of love,

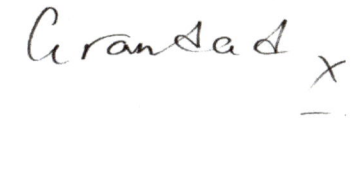

Grandad x

Painswick

April 2020

GRANDMA'S GOING NUTS

Grandma's going nuts, in isolation
Showing signs of severe frustration
Now, I can sit and read, basically do nowt
She cannot, and is desperate to go out!
But she can't go and join other folks
That most definitely – would be no joke.

Grandma's going nuts, in isolation
There's enough food to feed the nation
So, why are people panic-buying in the shops?
Latest updates – they're now out of Coco-Pops
Children have eaten every single box
That really is one of the biggest shocks!

Grandma's going nuts, in isolation
Not really such a surprising sensation,
She wants to go and meet her friends
And doesn't know, when she can again.
Can't go to College, pilates or the gym
I've just told her – she must stay in!

Grandma's going nuts, in isolation
Which has resulted in some revelations
She really can't do without her phone,
But is glad we're not alone

As we can regularly be in touch
Which of course, we value very much!

Grandma's going nuts, in isolation
She's reacting with high consternation
Just how long will this endure?
I don't think that I can take much more….

Grandma's going nuts, in isolation.
But she isn't giving in to the temptation
Should we stay in bed – and not get up?
No, we must arise and tidy up
Keep spirits high, standards maintain
It will surely help us – to stay sane!

Grandma's going nuts, in isolation
You know how much she loves org-an-i-sation
So she's telling me - exactly what to do
Just like Mum and Dad with you!
I suppose it's really for the best.
But I'm so busy – I just need a rest!!

Grandma's going nuts, in isolation
Amid concerns of de-forest-ation
Orang-utans are in turmoil
As farmers now grow plants for palm oil
They're surely losing all their natural habitat
And that, quite naturally, makes us very sad.

Grandma's going nuts, in isolation
But now I think she expects accreditation!
I'll have to draw a cert-if-i-cate

Life in Lockdown | 83

Out of 10, I'll give her 8!
For being, oh so very good……
That isn't natural, which is understood!

Grandma's going nuts, in isolation
This morning there was devastation
When from the bathroom came a scream!
Why? You ask – I'll tell you what I've seen.
The shower rail had fallen down
Grandma in said shower, not in her dressing gown…
So she had to wash under the tap
Before you ask, no, I didn't photo that!

Grandma's going nuts!

May 2020

THE STORY OF LEARNING TO DRIVE

As you know, I love my car. I like to keep it clean and tidy and therefore have very strict rules for my passengers. These are to ensure that I maintain the cleanliness of everything and that the interior remains in as pristine a condition as possible. Rules, in summary are, as follows:

- No eating

- No pumping

- No puking

Fortunately, most of the time everyone respects these requirements (2 out of 3 ain't bad!). Grandma has only just begun to comply with Rule Number 3, but I forgive her, as she suffers from travel sickness.

Most people take driving a car for granted. I do not. I never have. In fact, the thrill of being behind the wheel is still a "novelty" for me. Every time I go on a journey in the car, I am excited and I still am thrilled that I am actually able to drive. Why? I hear you ask. Well, I shall explain – are you sitting comfortably? (in the back, seat-belt on) and ready to go?!

At the age of 17, a frequent Birthday gift for teenagers, is a set of driving lessons, a pair of "L" plates and insurance for the family car. This last element is to enable Mum or Dad to help in the learning process, by taking their teenager out for "practice sessions". Most, if not all my friends and everyone I was at school with, experienced this "rite of passage" in 1976, when we all turned 17. It was a memorable year because it was a particularly hot summer, there was a drought, water rationing and as a result that year is oft-quoted as a happy, carefree time, despite economic problems of that period. For me, it was memorable for other reasons. I did not have driving lessons. I never even contemplated the possibility. I didn't feel as if I was missing out, quite simply because it never even occurred to me – for a single second – that I would ever be behind the wheel of a car. How could I? My right leg was weak and of course I had no use of my right hand. I don't remember what my parents did buy me for my Birthday, but the possibility of driving lessons never even entered my head. It was never mentioned – understandably.

The other memorable part of that glorious summer of 76 was that it marked my final operation in Alder Hey Children's Hospital in Liverpool. (of "Operation Ouch" fame, which is obviously why I love that programme so much!). I had been treated there all my life. I should, theoretically have been admitted to an "adult" hospital, as Alder Hey treated children up to the age of 16. It was agreed, however, that as I had been there for ever, the consultant was based there as a paediatric surgeon, I could have the operation there. It was to try and create a rotation movement. It didn't really work. After that I was told that the next option was to split the bicep. This would result in my right arm being straight, rather than sitting at half-mast across my tummy, as it does now – and always has. Because I was 17, it was my decision. I asked if the result would be any more movement, mobility or function. The answer was "no, not really". The next question was, "will it look better?" – you know what a vain creature I am! The answer to that was far more vague. "It will hang by your side, so people won't notice it stuck over your tummy. But it will be loose and floppy and you'll have no strength to carry anything over your arm". As I could, and can, carry a bag of shopping or a holdall over my arm, I thought that the end result could actually be a retrograde step. Also, it would have meant more time in hospital, more physiotherapy and more time away from school. I therefore said, "thanks, but no thanks. I have my A-Levels next year, I want to go to University, and if there is no ultimate benefit, then I don't think it is worthwhile". From that day to this, nothing has changed and I have never been back in hospital – thankfully!

THE STORY OF WAYNE

When I was in hospital, that summer, I spent several days on a children's ward – well of course I did, it was a children's hospital. As a 17 year old, it was a little bizarre to be surrounded by small kids. Actually, it was fine, because to them I seemed like a grown-up, and occasionally, I could help, if they were scared or upset for example. In the bed next door to me was a little boy. He was only 4 years old. His name was Wayne. He was a lovely little chap and despite being in hospital, was mostly very happy and very cheerful. We became good friends. "Why was *he* in hospital, Grandad?" I hear you ask. Well, if you remember, this was a really hot summer. The summer of 76 is mentioned a great deal. Now, when you are 4, and it is dead hot and dead sunny every single day, what is it that you want most in the world, as a treat? Yes, ice cream, of course!

Wayne, like every self-respecting little boy wanted an ice cream every single day, and he was allowed. He couldn't wait for the sound of the ice cream van to come down his street. Mr. Wippy, with the tinny tune of "Greensleeves" announcing his arrival. Such was Wayne's excitement, one day, clutching his 30p, he ran out of the house, didn't stop to look, as he was about to race across the road – and unfortunately he didn't see the van approaching. The ice cream man, driving his van, didn't see Wayne in time either. He hit him and sent Wayne (4 years old) flying. He had broken his leg very badly. An "ambliance" was called and he was rushed to Alder Hey, where he ended up in as ward, next to a "big boy", called John.

In those days, Mummy and Daddy were not allowed to visit their children in hospital at any time of day, as you are allowed to nowadays. Then, visits were between 6 and 7 o'clock in the evening. That was all. At 7.30 pm (remember it was a children's ward), we were put to bed and the lights went out. It didn't go dark until 9 o'clock (it was summer), but at 17, with the little children, I was put to bed!

I don't know where Wayne's Mummy was. I can't remember if he had a Mummy, but it was only his Daddy, who used to visit him every evening, for the full hour from 6 until 7. I suppose my Mum and Dad came to see me, I don't recall (and anyway this is the story of Wayne!). Now, every night, when the nurses asked visitors to leave, and Wayne's Daddy said, "Ta -ra Wayne" in a glorious Scouse accent, it was the only time when Wayne became upset. Daddy would say, "ta-ra Wayne", to which his delightful little boy would reply, "ta-ra Dad!". As he got to the entrance of the ward, this exchange would be repeated. As his Daddy disappeared, Wayne would sob, but he would continue to shout, "ta-ra Dad!", to which a distant, loud call would be heard "ta-ra Wayne". This continued, until Wayne's Daddy had gone, and there was no longer a "ta-ra Wayne" to be heard. Wayne would continue for a while, in the hope that magically, somehow, he would hear his Daddy's voice, or even better, his Daddy would re-appear at the door of the ward. At last, he would realise that Daddy was gone. The tears flowed. He was inconsolable for a little while. I would try to distract him, to comfort him, and as is always the case with a very small child, he allowed himself to be distracted. By "bedtime" at 7.30 he would be fine.

This scenario played out every night. When it was time for me to be discharged from Alder Hey, for the very last time – I was to be collected by my Father. You, Lucas and you Charlotte never knew my Father. He too comes / came from Liverpool. He did not speak with a Scouse accent. He was a very serious man. He would never say, "ta-ra", he would, naturally enough, only say, "Good-Bye". I packed my bag, which Dad carried for me. I said, "thank you and good-bye" to all the nurses. I then gave Wayne a hug, explained that I was going home and uttered the immortal words.....yes, you've guessed, "Ta-ra Wayne", to which he of course replied, "ta-ra John". I did the same at the entrance to the ward. My Father looked at me, didn't say anything, but I could tell that he was more than a little taken aback! As we walked along the corridor, I could hear the refrain, "ta-ra John", and I replied accordingly. For as long as I could, and knowing that he could still hear me, I shouted back, "ta-ra Wayne!", much to my Father's dismay. I had to – but I also knew the tears that would envelop my little friend, once he could no longer hear my voice, as the realisation dawned on him that I had gone. I wonder whatever happened to him – and I always, always cross the road carefully, especially if a 99 with a flake, raspberry ripple sauce and "hundreds&thousands" are involved!

I said that nothing has changed, or had changed since I left Alder Hey that day. One thing has changed though – the most incredible thing – I can drive a car!

The very first time I got behind the wheel of a car was in the summer of 1977. No, that is not when I learnt to drive. There wasn't a miracle revelation. It was my friend Donald, who allowed me to have a go in his Mum's brand new, yes brand new car – on the beach near his house! His Mum had bought a Leyland Daf "Variomatic" – rather like an automatic. It was a horrible "purple" colour, a box-shaped "sewing machine" on wheels, that was ugly, slow and very noisy. Donald of course, like so many others, had passed his driving test and his Mum allowed him to drive this brand new vehicle. He drove it onto the beach, where we used to go and walk his dogs (Angelina Birch and Charlie Brown Birch). The beach was empty, the tide was out and we were the only people there. As we about to leave, to go home, Donald suggested I try to drive along the beach for a bit. Why he thought of this, I have no idea. My immediate reaction was, "your Mum'll kill you" – if I didn't kill us first by driving into the sea (despite the tide being out!).

He reassured me that it wouldn't happen, it was dead easy, all you have to do is hold the steering wheel and press the pedal with one foot. So, hugely excited, hugely scared and with huge trepidation I got in the driver's side, Donald next to me. The engine was already running, he made sure I knew which pedal to press, he released the handbrake and said, "go". I was shaking so much, I could barely stop my legs shaking, the car juddered, moved forward a bit, making an awful noise (that was nothing to do with me) and carried on along the sand. I was really worried about hitting something (the beach was empty), or breaking the car – it was so basic, nothing could go wrong but still, I was petrified. We carried on for a little while but by then I had had enough. I stopped, Donald put the hand brake on – and we swapped seats. It was brilliant – and frightening – in equal measure. It also confirmed what I already knew – I would never, ever, be able to drive a car for real.

The years went by: I did my A Levels, went to university, travelled to France (by train and ferry!), lived in France, came back to England and trained as a teacher. When I was offered a job at Winchcombe School, I had to find somewhere to live, close by. Fortunately I found a "house share" with 3 other guys. I was able to walk to work – to school – every day. I had to get up early though, so that I could avoid walking up the road with all the children, my pupils. I was always at work before 8 am!!

Just before half-term of my very first term as a French teacher, there was an "outing" arranged for Y7 / Y8 pupils. It was a visit to the "Star Centre" just outside Cheltenham. That is a school and residential home for young people who have severe injuries from car accidents and those with disabilities. We were going to play wheelchair basketball with some children at the "home". It was fantastic to see the children – able-bodied and those with more limited mobility play together – as competitive as each other.

One of the carers was watching with me. We began chatting and he very proudly told me that he had recently met Princess Diana. She had been on a visit to Ullenwood, where the Star Centre is located. He had been introduced to her, because not only was he a carer, but he was also the driving instructor for residents who had reached the age of 17. I was incredulous. "Surely they can't drive?", said I, incredulously. "Yes, they can – of course they can", he replied, as if it were the most normal thing in the world. I can't have masked my amazement, because he then asked, "Can you drive then?", knowing very well, I suspect, what my answer would be, given my initial reaction to what he had told me. "No, of course not" I said. I didn't mention the beach episode in the Daf!

Roger, himself "disabled" from the ravages of tuberculosis, then uttered the most wonderful words. "I'll teach you John". I could barely believe my ears. I stared at him, dumb-struck for a few moments, and then I said, "Really? Are you sure? Are you being serious? Is that even possible?". He assured me that indeed it *was* possible, it would be a pleasure. He continued by pointing out some young people in wheelchairs, some part paralysed from car accidents, another with Muscular Dystrophy, explaining that they were learning to drive in his "adapted Mini". I was amazed. We agreed to be in touch, to make arrangements, so that he could give me driving lessons. Good to his word, after half-term, I took the bus from Winchcombe to Cheltenham, immediately the bell went at school, and he gave me my very first driving lesson, proper.

Just as on the beach, 6 years earlier, I was excited – and petrified – in equal measure. He could tell. Roger told me to try and relax – as if! He talked me through "the basics", he showed me the indicators, on the floor (two buttons drilled into the floor

– one for left, one for right turns), assured me that the steering ball was attached strongly enough to the steering wheel and then he drove to a very quiet, wide residential street. He pulled in, turned off the engine, and said, "Right, John, now your turn". He got out, I got out, we changed places. Wow – this was actually for real. I was soooo nervous. I was shaking like a leaf. When I'm scared, dead nervous or really stressed, my leg shakes uncontrollably, and it's a real struggle to make it stop. I sat there, looking at the controls, looking at the road and waiting for instructions. "Turn the key" – check. The car started. "Keep your left foot down on the brake pedal" – check. I was almost pushing it down onto the carpet. "Release the handbrake" – check. "Now lift your foot gently off the brake. As you do that, simultaneously apply a little pressure on the accelerator with your right foot". There was a cushion (a little like the ones you see in Church) on the floor under the accelerator, to raise my foot a little, so that it would be easier. I did everything he told me to. The car stuttered, jerked and moved forward a bit. It seemed to be shaking as much as I was. Roger then said some very "politically incorrect" things to me and used swear words (which I don't know Charlotte!) that I could not repeat here, and he used the dual controls to stop the car. He then laughed and told me that it is always like that, the very first time. He kept on swearing at me, making me laugh and eventually, to relax.

We had another go, and gradually, very gradually over a number of lessons, I managed to drive the car, albeit very slowly and very cautiously. At the start of every new lesson, I would be nervous, having forgotten everything I had been taught, or so I thought. One day, it all "clicked". I got in the car, I turned on the engine and I drove – without being nervous, without juddering the car, without "forgetting" everything. From that moment, I felt very much more confident. I had also met some of Roger's other pupils, far more disabled than I am. He would say to me, "if they can do it John, you sure as hell can". He was right. The Mini was a very small car in those days, his was always being cleaned because sometimes young people would have an accident and sometimes they actually had to be lifted from a wheelchair into the driving seat. It was very humbling and made me realise that Roger was right. The problems some of those teenagers had, were far worse than my restricted movement. I made progress and we put in for my Driving Test. This would be quite early in the New Year 1984. I wanted a car. I wanted a Mini – just like Roger's. My friend Derek helped me find one. Eventually, in the local newspaper, there was an ad for a 3 or 4 year old Mini (1980 reg if I remember). It had been owned by an old lady, she had looked after it, it had reasonably low mileage and I wanted it – the moment I set eyes on it. Derek, kindly, took it for a drive and assured me that it "sounded fine". No other checks, no other inspections – I bought it there and then. £2,000 – which I couldn't really afford, but I was so desperate to have it. Derek drove it home for me. I was soooo excited!

A couple of weeks after I had bought the Mini PAD 263 W – "Paddy" (you always give a name to your very first car!), I had my test. By this point, I thought I was not a bad driver. Unfortunately the Examiner thought otherwise. I failed. I can't remember exactly the reasons – but I was just too nervous on the day. It was THAT important to me.

I was so disappointed and ashamed almost, as I gave Roger the news. He consoled me, but also, in brutally honest terms, told me that I had not been ready for the test. Not that I couldn't drive and do all the necessary manoeuvres, but that I was too "emotional"; he had known that I would shake, worry and fail! He told me to take a total break from driving. He assured me that I would not forget everything. He told me that he would take it up again, after the Easter Holidays. I agreed, but made him promise not to forget!

As agreed, after a 2 month break, and once I was back at school after Easter, we began to have lessons – sometimes twice a week. I would use his Mini, because it had dual controls, just in case. By this time, I had had my Mini adapted, so that the indicators were buttons on the floor, just like Roger's. The holes were not as tidy or as watertight, but they worked and it was exactly what I was used to by then. I also had a "cushion" exactly like his, under my right foot, for comfort and to prevent my leg from becoming too tired.

Progress was swift. All anxiety seemed to have evaporated. The 2 month break had been exactly what I needed. Roger still swore at me, we laughed together and became very good friends. I applied for a second attempt at the Driving Test. It would happen in Cheltenham. I had practised the route, as everyone does, and spent hours driving around the streets (just like we see lots of learner drivers in Pinelands Way near your house). I was ready. I received a letter, to inform me of the date: Monday 24th July 1984.

"Why can you remember that, Grandad?" (you sad old man), I hear you ask. Well, I am a bit like that, as you know – remembering daft stuff which is of no importance whatsoever. The actual reason I remember is because it was the very first day of the School Summer Holidays. All I could think about was the possibility of seeing one of the children I taught, in town, as I was doing the test – or even worse – if they saw me! Fortunately all went well – and I did pass my Driving Test – 36 years ago. I was so happy, so proud, sooooo relieved!!

Now, I could drive my very own car, wherever, whenever I chose – what freedom! I can physically remember the sensation, when I first drove at 60 mph. I'm not sure who was more pleased – me or the car! On the road between Cheltenham and Oxford, where it is straight and the limit is 60. I love that road. It is part of the route, when we go to Cotswold Wildlife Park. The very first time I did it on my own, in my own car and reached 60 mph I was exhilarated. It was the most wonderful moment. Even now, 36 years later, when I drive that route, even when you are in the back of my A3 and Grandma is sitting next to me, I know the exact spot where I experienced that huge feat of speed for the very first time. Every time it still gives me a huge thrill to remember that exact moment.

Of course, I had passed my test but this did not mean that I could drive! The skill of being on the road, aware of other drivers, going on the motorway, into "unknown territory" for the first time is really frightening. You make mistakes. I did.

Although I loved that car – still do – by the time I part-exchanged it – for a Metro – there was not one single original panel, that had been left unscarred – including the roof! No, I didn't roll the motor – but one New Year's Eve, when I was in Edinburgh to celebrate Hogmanay, the Mini was parked overnight, outside the flat where I was staying. On New Year's Day, when I went outside, I could see two large indentations on the roof, over the driver's side and the passenger side, at the front of the car. There were also two huge footprints on the bonnet. Some late-night reveller had decided they needed a "wee sit down" on their way home from a New Year's Eve party. What better place than the roof of my car – ugh! That was never "repaired" as such; I simply got inside and punched out the bum cheek marks, as best I could.

I still had the car when I met Grandma. I still loved my car and loved driving it as often as possible. Grandma didn't like it. Grandma thought it was too small. Grandma thought it was too slow. Grandma thought that there were too many shades of beige, as each panel was slightly different from the original colour, but did not match each other exactly. But I loved my car. I loved the fact that I could drive. I still love the fact that I, I CAN DRIVE. The novelty is still there every, every time, that I get inside my car. I am still thrilled that I, who never imagined that I would be able to drive, can drive, have a nice car, and that is why I like to keep it clean and tidy and why in my car – it is my rules.

THE STORY OF BRECON

When I was a teacher, one of the highlights of the school year was "activity week". This took place near the end of the summer term, once all the exams had been taken, reports were written and we were all (teachers and children!) in a state of heightened anticipation of the holidays.

For Y7 and Y8, there were days out locally. As the school was in a very small town and nestled in the rolling Cotswold Hills, it was easy to head out, with a picnic, to discover the surrounding countryside. As the children often knew the landscape better than the teachers, it was tremendous fun and also very informative. During my first year there, and because my Tutor Group was Y8, I spent a very happy week, traipsing around the area – a really pleasant way to spend the final days of term.

For Y9 though, that week of the year was the pinnacle of excitement. The anticipation, the stories, the expectations, the sheer excitement rose with every passing day, from the start of the summer term onwards. All the children could think about, every conversation they had was centred on "Brecon". This referred to the Brecon Beacons, in South Wales. The Headteacher had a tiny "holiday cottage" hidden away in a beautifully isolated valley, just outside Brecon. The Head of Science, Mr. Williams was a Welshman, and therefore several years before I joined the school, a camping trip to the Brecon Beacons had been arranged and had become a permanent fixture of the school calendar.

Tales of "Brecon" became "folklore" almost. The children though, were sworn to secrecy, so that the following year's pupils would not have any surprises spoilt, by hearing about what happened "on camp". I suppose it is like the saying about Las Vegas, only transferred to South Wales – "what happens in Brecon, stays in Brecon!". Even younger brothers or sisters were not told (supposedly!) about the adventures that everyone had "down the valley".

I too, became fascinated by all the wonderful stories, reminiscences in the staffroom from those colleagues who led the trip to Wales. Like the children, I too desperately wanted to go and experience it all for myself! Then, in my second year as a teacher, when the planning for "activity week" began, I was asked by Mr. Williams if I wanted to go – I almost bit his arm off! I'm not sure who was more excited – the kids or Mr. Parsons!!

The trip was from Monday morning, when the coaches left school and we returned in time for the bell on Friday afternoon. What I had forgotten though, was the need to put up all the tents. We hired a huge marquee, that was erected for us by a local company, but the "Scout" tents that we used, had to be put up – by the teachers.

We filled the school mini-bus with all the paraphernalia, mallets, guy ropes, tents, groundsheets, and probably lots of other gubbins, long since forgotten, but I was delighted to be part of the team going to Brecon. We, a group of 6, set off on the Friday evening and drove to the campsite. Although it was the first time for me, for the other teachers it was a well - established routine. (The words, "we always do….." come to mind, Lucas!). We drove through Abergavenny, whose football team, famously, is Abergavenny Thursdays – not Sheffield Wednesday! As we approached the campsite, right next to a river, I saw Mr. Partridge's car – "that's weird", I thought. How did that get here? He was the Headteacher and he had driven to his holiday home and had come to meet us. We had a lovely evening, made a barbecue, had a few beers and chatted long into the night. The other teachers talked about the programme for the week, the children who'd be there, the characters, the scaredy cats, those who would miss home and so on. I listened intently, especially to the programme. Mr. Williams said, "I shan't forget the iron!". I didn't dare ask, but I thought to myself, "why on earth do we need an iron for a camping trip? We won't be pressing our trousers or needing to get creases out of our shirts".

The following morning, we cracked on with the task of putting up all the tents. The local company arrived, to erect the marquee. We showed them exactly where it had to go. It was fascinating to watch how such a huge structure, poles, ropes, tarpaulin, canvas and enormous metal pegs, very quickly took shape. Once everything was finished, we got back into a now empty mini-bus and headed back to school. We arrived early on Saturday evening, to have Sunday packing, before setting off on Monday morning, with two coachloads of kids!!

The journey was really noisy. Everyone was chatting excitedly – all sorts of exaggerated tales from youngsters who explained what they had *definitely, 100% (ja!)* been told about what happened at Brecon. None of it was true, it was just nervous, hilarious banter, and we the teachers happily allowed the children to speculate (wildly) about the days to come.

As a "newbie" myself, when we arrived, I followed the lead of Mr. Williams and the other members of staff. We had, in advance, allocated children to specific tents, ensuring that friendship groups were respected, as far as poss, and making sure that the girls' tents were away from the boys' tents. Nobody moaned (they had been warned not to!). Once they were all unpacked and settled, everyone had tasks, to help prepare the evening meal. Dead excited! There were rotas established, by tent, for washing up, drying and putting away all the utensils, beakers and plates. As it was the beginning of July, there was sufficient light to organise some games and as tradition dictated a rope swing was erected from a tree on the opposite bank of the river. At 10 o'clock, everyone went to bed. Well, they went into their tents. As ever, for the first night, everyone was soooo excited, that nobody got to sleep right away. This is normal, this is part of the fun at camp. That said, if Y9 pupils have no sleep, then the next day they are going to be very grumpy, very tired and probably very uncooperative. For a while, the teachers, me included, would go round, now with a torch, asking everyone to settle down. This continued for a while, until another "tradition" of Brecon came to pass.

Mr. Williams went to the noisiest tent (boys), opened the flap and hauled one boy out. At a volume, so that the entire camp could hear, he uttered the immortal words, "David – I have told you to go to sleep, haven't I?". "Yes Sir".

"If you do not go to sleep, tomorrow morning you will not be a happy bunny. You need to be bright-eyed and bushy-tailed don't you? What do you need to be in the morning, David?" "Bright-eyed and bushy-tailed Sir". "Correct, my boy. Therefore, get back in your tent, get back into your sleeping bag and get to sleep –

got it?" "Yes Sir". And from that point on, camp was quiet. We stayed up and took it in turns to patrol the tents, just to make sure everyone was fine, not poorly, not homesick and not scared. There were always 2 teachers "on duty" throughout the night. The children were told that if there really was a problem, they were allowed to fetch a teacher. It very rarely happened and we hardly ever had to tell anyone off, for being daft, too noisy or too naughty.

Tuesday was orienteering around the surrounding countryside. Teams setting off at suitable intervals with clues, coordinates, compass, map and "rations". This was great fun and we, the teachers were strategically positioned around the course, so that nobody was ever really too far away or out of range. Fortunately we never lost anybody!

Wednesday was always a highlight. We brought back the coaches and we all drove to the Mumbles. This is a stretch of seaside, just outside Swansea. Some children had never seen the sea – ever! It was a brilliant time, playing, swimming, digging, chasing, football, cricket and catch on the beach – pretty much all day long. We were blessed with fine weather, warm sunshine and everyone had a wonderful time. Rather than go back to camp and begin cooking an evening meal, as a real treat we had fish and chips, bought at a "chippie" on the front in Mumbles. It must have taken ages to organise (did we order in advance? I can't remember, but think that we must have). That meal was always a great success as we all tucked into let's face it, what is everyone's (fantasy) favourite meal.

Thursday was the big day – the reason we were actually in Brecon. We were all to climb Pen y Fan – the highest peak in the Brecon Beacons, at almost 3,000 feet. Our campsite was in Cryb Coch, on the slopes of the start of the climb. It would take all day and everyone was going to "get up that mountain", as Mr. Williams would tell us, before we set off. As with any group of people, some were more "keen" than others. There were those who wanted to "hare off" into the distance, as quickly and as fast as poss – others who would look up, at what seemed in their eyes to be Mount Everest, and say, "there's no way, I can't do that". I was always with the weakest group – the "stragglers". This suited me, because I am not that strong, and I was able to encourage the slower children to make steady progress. "Sir, I can't go no further" (I quote), was an oft-repeated moan. There was one tactic that always helped those who were struggling that they could, indeed manage and that they would be able to "get up that mountain". I would stop and say, "Listen, you walk, carry on up, as slowly as you need,. and after one minute, I shall shout up to you and you'll be able to see just how far you've gone, in just ONE minute". "But Sir…." "Just do it, Bryony". "I can't". "Go on, slow steady steps, I promise I'll call after 60 seconds". Reluctantly, she – and others – trudged off, as if they were about to collapse. After the allotted minute, I would call. They'd look back, amazed at the distance they'd covered (not that much really, but it looked as if it were). I'd say, "well done", let them wait for me to catch up and then set off again, using the same tactic, if needed. Often just once or twice was sufficient. Slowly but surely, we would carry on – and always – absolutely always – every child made it to the summit. The sense of achievement for each and every one of them was delightful to witness. Truth be told, I was pretty chuffed with myself too! The views are superb and one can spend a little time on the plateau that comprises the summit. Eventually though, you have to meander down, back towards camp. There is a slightly longer route, whereby you make a large arc to go around the lower slopes. Everybody is so elated, and going down seems so much easier, that very often groups would follow the longer track.

There is a story about the very place where we camp, a true story – from 1900. We camp by the river at Cwmllwch (kumlok), at the very start of the climb up this side of Pen y Fan. The remains of a cottage can still be seen, a little way up the hillside from our camp. Here is what happened, over 100 years ago…

On 4 August 1900 a miner from Maerdy, at the head of the Rhondda Fach valley, decided to take his five-year-old son Tommy to visit his grandparents who still farmed near Brecon. They'd travelled by train and planned to walk the four miles to Cwmllwch, the farmhouse in the valley just below Pen y Fan.

A LONG JOURNEY

By 8pm they'd reached the Login - now in ruins - where soldiers were encamped for training at the rifle range further up the valley at Cwm Gwdi. The father and son had stopped for refreshment when they met Tommy's grandfather and cousin William, who was 13. William was asked to go back to the farm and tell his grandmother to expect Tommy and his dad, and Tommy ran off up the valley with him.

When the two boys were halfway, Tommy who was frightened by the dark perhaps, started to cry and wanted to return to his father at the Login. So the two boys parted. William completed his errand and returned to the Login within a quarter of an hour – but Tommy hadn't returned.

MISSING

His father and grandfather started the search immediately, joined by soldiers from the camp. The search was halted at midnight and resumed at 3pm the following day. The search continued for weeks. Every day, parties of police, soldiers, farmers and other volunteers systematically combed the area with no luck.

THE DREAM

After reading accounts of the search, a gardener's wife living just north of Brecon is said to have dreamed of the very spot where Tommy was found. She had a few restless days before persuading her husband to borrow a pony and trap on Sunday 2 September to take her and some relatives to Brecon Beacons, which they'd never climbed before.

They reached the ridge below Pen y Fan and were making their way towards the summit over open ground when Mr Hammer, who was a few yards in front, started back with an exclamation of horror. He had found the body of little Tommy Jones.

MEMORIAL

No one could explain how the five-year-old had managed to reach the spot where his body was found. He'd climbed 1,300ft from the Login. Today the spot where Tommy's body was found is marked with an obelisk. The jurors at the inquest donated their fees after determining that he had died from exhaustion and exposure.

Of course, we would tell the children the story of Tommy Jones, normally during the descent, as we passed the obelisk. We also at that point explained the significance of the tumbled-down cottage, a little way up the hill, from camp. We might have suggested that the ghost of the little boy, and all the people out on the mountainside looking for him, could be seen – or heard - at night, when it was dark, the trees were rustling, the wind blowing, the shadows cast by the moon on the rock formations……..

Everyone believed the story – well the story of the little boy is true – and there was always someone, or a group of them, that would believe the story of the ghost. That night, we could always tell which tent was most spooked. There would be torches, after "lights out" and lots of whispering, shrieks and then voices saying, "Did you hear that?" "What was that?" "I'm sure I heard something" "Over there" and so on. We, the teachers thought this was dead funny. As it was the last night, and everyone really was exhausted, having climbed Pen y Fan, we didn't tell anyone off, or try and make them go to sleep. We knew it would happen – soon enough – once all the ghost stories had been told.

Everyone had to be really early on Friday morning – our last day, We had to pack, take down the tents, clean up the site and be ready for the coaches to collect us, to take us home, in time for the bell at the end of the school day.

The routine, as with everything at Brecon was well-established and very well executed. The children were told that they had to be up, washed and packed as quickly as possible. All of their belongings, day sacks as well as sleeping bags and rucksacks needed to be out of the tent and placed in the marquee by 8.30.

Everything went like clockwork. There were always children who had "lost" stuff – socks gone, a washbag "borrowed" or "lent" to someone, a sleeping bag cover that had mysteriously disappeared – forever – from inside a confined space of a ten man tent.......finally the tents were empty. A pupil from each tent then "volunteered" to brush the groundsheet – mud, grass, sweets, wrappers, toothpaste, water...... but they were always very good at cleaning it all out.

Everyone, about 90 children, would gather round one of the teachers' tents. This was so that they could be shown how to take down the tent, and in what order to complete each part of this delicate exercise. Mr. Williams would explain everything very clearly and as he explained the process, repeated it, as he and we other teachers, obeyed his commands, to ensure the tent was dismantled correctly. The groundsheet would be removed – check. Two people would fold it – check. Then the pegs would be removed – check. You would make sure to leave them in their exact position on the ground next to the tent – check. Someone would collect them, and count the exact number – check. That same person would then put the pegs in the peg bag, one for each tent – check. Then the guy ropes – check. The poles – check. And so on. At the end of the entire process, the canvas would be lying on the ground. "At that point", said Mr. Williams. "you stand by your beds and you await further instructions – what do you do, ladies and gentlemen?" and there would be a chorus, from everyone, "we stand by our beds and await further instructions Sir". "Very good", said Mr. W.

The children would then go to their tent, do all the necessary tasks, with us helping, showing, reminding where necessary, but all in all, it worked really well and after a while each group of children would be standing next to their tent, by this time on the ground. Each had a mallet, a bag of pegs, a set of poles – all ready to be packed away – and a tent to fold. Once everyone had finished, at a given signal....

Mr. Jones, the Geography teacher – a genuinely hilarious man – would say to Mr. Williams, "Excuse me Mr. Williams, what about all the creases in these tents?". "Ah, thank you for reminding me, Mr. Jones. Yes, the creases. That is always a problem. Listen everyone. Before we put the tents away, we have to get rid of the creases". Mr. Jones would reply, "I did remember to bring the iron with me, Mr. Williams, shall I fetch it from the minibus?" "Would you? Yes please Mr. Jones".

So, Bob, (Mr. Jones) would go over to the bus, go into the glove box and remove a package. The children would be standing, incredulous – surely this can't be right…. ironing the tents? The box was a genuine box that had once contained a brand new steam iron. Not now though…..

Mr. Jones would hand over the box to Mr. Williams. With great ceremony, he would lay it on the ground, next to his feet, and say, "we need a volunteer. I will give instructions, but someone has to demonstrate how best to remove the creases from the tent, to show everyone what needs to be done". He would then select a child – (someone, we the teachers had agreed in advance, who had a great sense of humour, would not be upset and would not be ridiculed by his classmates for what was about to unfold – pardon the pun).

"Charlie", he would say, "well done my boy, you are my volunteer". The chosen pupil would come forward. Mr. Williams told him to kneel on the tent, near the edge and straighten out the first section with his hands. "That makes it easier to iron, you see". That done, Mr. Williams would then pick up the box – and remove the iron. It was a toy iron, bright red plastic. Everyone would look for a moment, in silence, not quite able to take in, what they were looking at. They began to laugh. "SSSHHH please everyone". The iron was handed to Charlie and he began to iron the tent, using what everyone could see was a toy! Another teacher would quickly take a photo, the iron taken off Charlie, he roared with laughter, we would all join in and the final tradition of Brecon had been respected. The children were sworn to secrecy, so that the same trick could be played the following year and every subsequent year! Fortunately we always chose a pupil who saw the funny side, was not humiliated or upset – everyone always kept the secret – until now.

THE END

June 2020

THE STORY OF WHY I BECAME A TEACHER

As a child, I did not particularly like school. Although I was good at some subjects, I was totally rubbish at others. Also, I was no good at sport, understandably. Furthermore, I missed quite a lot of lessons, when I was in hospital, or had to go for "check-ups" or physiotherapy at Alder Hey.

When you grow up, there are elements of your childhood that remain fixed in your memory. I remember very clearly my very first day at Primary School. My "girlfriend", Lynn, was locked in the cupboard by Miss Addshead, because she was crying so much! I have a vivid memory of the "hopping race" that I was allowed to take part in, even though my right leg was in plaster – I came second!

The first day at David House is clearly imprinted on my mind. Lining up in the playground, as our names were called and being led into Form 1. I can see myself now, sitting on the floor of Miss Barrow's study, learning my spellings, as part of Prep Class.

There are other recollections, which remain with me, as important moments of those school days. My first week learning French, for example. By Friday, I knew that I wanted to "do French". From that point on, whenever any adult, agèd aunt or any other well-meaning relative asked the question, "What do you want to do when you grow up John?", the answer was always, "French". I didn't know what I would do with "French", I just knew that, during the very first week, I had discovered something that just "clicked", it made sense, I enjoyed it, I could remember it and I liked my teacher. That in itself was a little bizarre, because he was a very stern, serious man, who seemed quite scary to us – a class of small boys. Mr. Roxburgh always wore a bow tie, a tweed suit, had a very impressive moustache – and no arms. He had prosthetic limbs, but in the 1960s these were rather "rudimentary". At the elbow, or where his elbow should have been was a "light switch", which he could click, in order to straighten his arm. Occasionally, he would be sitting at his desk, and he would suddenly flick the switch on his arm, to become straight, the limb would immediately shoot into the fully extended position, as he pointed at some boy, who had done something wrong. I learned later, that he was in fact, a war hero. He had lost his arms in a vain attempt to stop a hand grenade from going off. It had landed close by him and his men. He tore off his helmet, to try and cover the device before it exploded. He wasn't quite fast enough……

The school had an excellent reputation for science, was strong in sports and had a very active Combined Cadet Force (playing soldiers). None of these were my forté, so it made sense to go to another school for 6th Form, one which had a good reputation for Modern Languages.

Just after my "O" Levels, (GCSE) but before I left at the end of the summer term, I was at Church Youth Club one Sunday evening. There was to be a talk about a project that would be taking place over the Summer Holidays. Audrey Humphreys and John Tomkins gave a presentation, explaining that they wanted to recruit teenagers, to help look after children from immigrant families during the school hols. My friends were not impressed and not keen on the idea. For some reason, it rather appealed to me. At the end, therefore, I approached Audrey and told her that I was very interested and would like to know more.

She explained that a group of children, who during term time were at the Crown Street Language Centre in Liverpool 8 (a poor area), needed people to look after them in the summer. They would be based in Paddington Comprehensive (a huge school in the city centre) where the facilities could be used, and that days out, locally, for the children, would also be organised. It sounded really good.

As preparation, there was a training weekend away, at Edge Hill, a Teacher Training College, near Liverpool. I attended that weekend, had a great time, learnt a great deal and met some very nice people. Many of them became very good friends, to this day; and indeed some of them would be in the 6th Form at my new school, in the September! One was Kathy, Audrey's daughter, who died more than 10 years ago. Another was Donald, (yes, the same Donald!), Jane, Joy, Elaine and Helen. All of those 4 girls would be at Quarry Bank, my new school!

PROJECT TO STOP 'CULTURE SHOCK'

More than 80 of Liverpool's immigrant schoolchildren are striving to overcome the "culture shock" on a three-week course at Paddington Comprehensive School.

They are taking part in a language enrichment project run during the school summer holidays.

The children, whose ages range from five to fifteen, come from countries as distant and varied as Bangladesh, Persia, India and Hong Kong.

A band od 40 voluntary workers, of schoolteachers, college students and sixth formers, will take the children on outings to North Wales and excursions round Liverpool with the aim of improving their spoken English and integrating them socially.

Liverpool Echo - July 1975, Summer School"

The summer holidays were great fun! In those days there was no "Health and Safety" and I wasn't really "qualified" – none of us were – to look after little kids, with a not very good command of English. It didn't matter. We played in the school grounds, we went to the park, we even took them swimming! One little boy, Winston, had a woolly swimming costume. As soon as he got in, the "cozzie" became very soggy and just fell off. He was a skinny scrap of a kid, so any swimming trunks would have been loose, but a sopping wet piece of wool had no chance! One day, Donald and I took a group of children on the bus. We went to my house, to collect our dog – a King Charles Spaniel called Tony. On the bus ride, of course we had to go upstairs – at the front – and the children for some reason started "singing" – Donald Duck, Donald Duck, which they thought was dead funny – so did Donald and I, though I suspect the other passengers did not!

In the 6th Form, there was a scheme whereby we could, if we wanted, go into Y7 and Y8, to help younger children read. I decided to be a part of that and really enjoyed it. Every Wednesday afternoon, for an hour, I would go to another site, and spend time with small groups of boys and girls, who were trying to improve their reading.

My desire to "do French" never wavered. I therefore went to University to study French Literature. It was a 4 year course, the third year of which was to be spent in France. The options were to study at a French university, or to teach in a French school. You know what I chose, don't you?! The "job title" is "assistant", someone to do conversation classes with French pupils. I got a job at a huge Secondary School – Lycée – in Abbeville, a city in northern France. I lived in the school, and because it was sooooo enormous, I was actually expected to teach the curriculum. Therefore, rather than doing short sessions with small groups of students, I had to actually teach – an hour at a time – to prepare the teenagers for the Baccalauréat – the equivalent of A Levels! The first lesson of the day started at 8 am! That was tough. I had to prepare lessons, teach grammar, structure, vocabulary – everything. I'd had no training, no real preparation and standing up in front of a class of 15, 16 or 17 year olds was quite daunting – I was only 20 myself! Being "dropped in the deep end" meant that I had to learn very quickly! Although I wasn't trained, I did understand grammar, knew about languages and because I had studied Latin, Ancient Greek (2 years!), French and German, I instinctively knew what it was like to have to learn the tenses, the vocabulary, the grammar – and I managed to keep my head above water!

It worked and I really enjoyed it. Again, it "clicked" and I thought, "I can do this". There was only one problem. One day, I was walking across the grounds to the block where I was to teach. One of the "proper" French teachers, saw this young person strolling across the grounds, where pupils were not allowed and shouted at me to move off and report to him at break. I had to run back and explain that I WAS a teacher, not a pupil. That is how large the school was – the guy didn't even know who I was!

My parents came to see me towards the end of that school year. They had been to the Loire Valley for a business trip by my Dad and they drove back to England, via Abbeville. They stayed in the nicest hotel in town and we had dinner in a lovely restaurant. Afterwards, I told them that I had decided to become a teacher, but that I was very worried. They were pleased to hear that I had made such a decision but were concerned about my "misgivings". I explained that my fear was that if children failed, then it would be my fault and that I didn't think I would be able to cope with that "guilt". My Father, very wisely said, "it won't necessarily be your fault". He then proceeded with the following analogy. It sustained me throughout my teaching career and in many other situations too. He said, "many people choose to become a doctor. They have patients who are ill. Sometimes those patients will die, however good the doctor is, who is treating them. It isn't the doctor's fault. They may be the best doctor in the world, but the patient just can't get better. The same applies to teachers". It was the best advice he ever uttered. It reassured me and reinforced my belief that I should become a teacher.

After my year in Abbeville came to an end, I went to Paris for a few days. I stayed with an English teacher from the Lycée, who had an apartment right in the heart of the city. It had been in her family for generations. Her Father used to work in "Les Halles", which in former days had been the central fruit and vegetable market for the whole of Paris and the surrounding area. It is now "Forum Les Halles", a huge shopping mall. I and another assistant from Abbeville had been to stay on a number of occasions throughout the school year. We would spend the weekend there – what a wonderful way to discover such a glorious city, based right in the heart of things – everything on the doorstep. Finally, I had to head to the Gare du Nord, for my train back to England. I had no job for the summer, as I had decided not to work on "colonies de vacances" again. Having taught for a year, I wanted to continue in that vein. At the station, I bought an English newspaper. It was a Tuesday. It was the "Guardian". I know this because the Guardian used to have advertisements for teaching jobs every Tuesday. I quickly turned to that page and scanned the ads – not really expecting to find anything – I was just "killing time" until I could board the "boat train". It was called that, not because when it arrived at the English Channel (la Manche as the French say), it entered the water, inflated lilos on the wheels and floated across the sea – it was because it was the train that connected with the ferry back to Dover. I digress.

There was an ad that caught my eye. It was for a summer job, as an ELT teacher (English Language Teaching) at a summer school that would take place in Cheltenham. I wondered where that was exactly. I'd heard of the town, but had never been and would have struggled to pinpoint it exactly on a map. It was to teach teenagers from across Europe, who would be on "holiday" in England, to learn English. Lessons in the morning, activities in the afternoon; it appealed, but I was not officially a teacher. I had nothing to lose though. Therefore, there and then, right away, immediately, as quickly as I could, (does that convey how enthusiastic I was?) found a phone box and rang the telephone number. It was answered by Peter Mullins. He was the Director of the Summer School. He was also a lecturer at the college where the school would be based. (It is now part of the University of Gloucestershire). I explained who I was, why I was calling, and wondered whether he would consider my application, even though I was not a fully qualified teacher. I wasn't qualified at all, but I didn't express it like that. I told Peter about my experience (a full year in a Lycée). He seemed interested. He asked me to travel to Cheltenham, once I was back in the UK, we could meet, and, making no promises, no guarantees, he would consider me for that summer.

I went to Cheltenham by train. We met. We got on. He agreed that I could work for a "fortnight" as a trial. He would then see whether I could *actually* teach, and if I was good enough, I could stay for the rest of the season. I jumped at the chance and was dead pleased! The rest, as the saying goes, "is history". This was summer 1980. Therefore 40 years since I arrived in the Cotswolds. One way or another I have been here ever since! The fortnight turned from 2 weeks into 2 months! I came back in 81 and 82!

Summer school was great fun. I taught groups of young people, some a little younger, some the same age as me. There were students from Croatia (it was still part of Yugoslavia in those days), whom I became close friends with. In subsequent years, I went to visit them in Zagreb as well as in Split (but that is another story!). The afternoon activities comprised of sports, "discovering the architecture of Cheltenham", going to Stratford – and the best of all, for me, taking a group of Germans to the Cricket Festival! Gloucestershire play 3 county matches and 2 "one dayers" in the grounds of Cheltenham College every July. So, I got to be there, paid, ticket paid for and all I had to do, was explain "ze rulez" ! Now, as you know Lucas, cricket is dead easy to understand. Once you play, or watch "very carefully", it all makes perfect sense – to an Englishman! Not so, for a teenage German! "Ze kwestionz" came zick und fast" "Vy is he out"? "Vot is a vikit?" "Vot is a zird Mann – zere are elefen". "Ven ze Mann comes out, vy iz he ze next Mann in?" "Und wenn he is out, vy does he go back in?" – did I see much cricket? Nein!

I stayed with a family, who were one of many host families to students or the accompanying adults, who came with each group. I was with Lesley and Derek – yes, the Derek from "learning to drive". They are still my very good friends. They were at our wedding! Their children, Richard and Claire are now about the same age as your Mum and Dad. I used to read them bedtime stories, taught Claire her tables – and she married a boy I taught at Winchcombe – small world!

As you know, I worked during the summer holidays on "colonies de vacances". I loved that. During my final year at University, I applied to become a "lecteur" at a University in France. It is the same "concept" as "assistant" in a school, but obviously at a much higher level in a University. I lived in Rouen, a beautiful city in Normandy. Again, however, it wasn't a "soft option". There were 4 of us – one from Liverpool University (moi), Evan – from Edinburgh University (Best Man at Grandma and my Wedding), Alison from Reading and Steve from Southampton University. The Head of Department organised it, so that we taught specific classes, mostly reading and written comprehension as well as the "conversation" classes. What we didn't realise was that we would be setting – and marking – the year-end exams for those students at the end of their second year of study. They had to pass all sections: literature, history, speaking, reading comprehension, translation, (French to English as well as English to French), and if they failed ANY element, then they had to re-sit the entire year. Yikes, what a responsibility! There was only one student we had to fail – Véronique. This was a real shame, because she had become a friend of ours. However painful, we could not allow her to pass.

At the end of that academic year (82), I knew that I was off to Cheltenham again for July and August, to do my stint with Peter, staying with Lesley and Derek. I had organised to be in London all September, to take an ELT course, to give me a proper qualification. Over the summer, I also thought about Modern Languages. Perhaps I should consider a PGCE – the qualification to become a French teacher in secondary schools in this country. I had done no research, not made any applications at all. I was in Cheltenham. I thought to myself, "where is the nearest University?". The answer was Bristol. So, I rang them up. I had a conversation with John Lees, the Head of the Modern Languages Department and he invited me for an interview. That went well, I had teaching experience, knew that I enjoyed being in front of a classroom and the clincher was my answer to the question – a trick question – "so, it is really good then, John, if everyone's quiet, writing everything down and studying hard?" "NO", I replied. "It has to be noisy – it has to be active – it has to be lots of interaction!". They could tell that I meant this, that I really believed it. They offered me a place, to start in October 1982 (after my month in London). Perfect! I was sooo delighted. Bristol had a great reputation and I was extremely excited at the prospect……

London was brilliant. Really, really hard work, but so stimulating, so challenging and so interesting. I learnt a great deal. Every day we had lessons, and then late afternoon we had to teach a class of foreign students. Every lesson had to be planned, delivered (while being watched and marked by my tutor), reviewed and analysed. I was exhausted and exhilarated in equal measure. I passed! The course was run by "International House". They instruct teachers like me, and they also run schools all over the world. They have a fantastic reputation. Immediately I had passed, I was offered a 1 year contract at International House Pamplona, in Spain. I was torn! I was so inspired by the course, I was flattered because I'd been offered a job, but I also had my course in Bristol to look forward to. I couldn't decide what to do. I sat on the stairs (a beautiful wooden staircase) in the reception of the building in Piccadilly, London and discussed my dilemma with my tutor, Martin. It so happened that he too had a PGCE from Bristol! He said that he understood my desire to shoot off immediately to Spain, but that Bristol would be brilliant too. At the end of a year in Bristol, I would have 2 qualifications – one for England, the other for the rest of the world! At that point, with both certificates "in my pocket", I could do anything I wanted. He was so right. I set off for Bristol, convinced that I had made the right decision. I had!

My Dad and I - Abbeville 1980

I enjoyed the course and taught in a wide range of schools. The second term was spent in its entirety in one school – "Teaching Practice". It was tough but good. The school was KLB – in Wotton-under-Edge, not far from where we now live!

At the end of the third term, I began to apply for a job – in England. Everybody was doing the same. As I had loved KLB so much, I decided to focus on Gloucestershire. As luck would have it, I managed to secure 3 interviews – bizarrely, all in the same week – Monday in Gloucester, another on Wednesday and bizarrely, one on Friday in Egremont in the Lakes!

On Monday I travelled to the King's School in Gloucester. The interview went well. The Headmaster, Reverend David was charming, and it really appealed. I would be obliged to do some "boarding duties" and Saturday school – not a problem – I'd had Saturday school until I was 16. Once the interview was finished, he then "relaxed" and asked me about "my school". It turned out that David House, my Prep School, had been his family home, when he was a little boy! His Father, Bishop David of Liverpool had donated the house to the school, decades before. What a coincidence! I think that part of the reason I had been invited for interview, was so that he could chat about his childhood home! I suspect that the classroom for Form 1 had been his nursery!! He sent me on my way, thanking me, telling me that I had done very well and that he "would be in touch". As there were other applicants to be seen on other days, I didn't expect to hear from him immediately. That said, I had two more interviews that very week. As I travelled back to Bristol on the train, I began to reflect and think very seriously about the day. I was flattered to have been interviewed, I performed with confidence, there was the "Liverpool link", but gradually doubts began to surface…it was a "rugby school", it was a "choir" school….sport and singing, as I've said and as you know all too well – are not my forté. If I were to be offered the job, did I really want it – did I really, really want it? It dawned on me that there were some cons – to counterbalance the pros…..ugh, what would I do? As the question had not arisen, I tried to put it out of my mind. I couldn't. I arrived home to my flat and explained everything to my landlady and her husband. He was a Professor of History at the university and she was a teacher, so they were interested in my dilemma. Later in the evening, the phone rang. Maureen answered it. My worst fear was confirmed….it was the Reverend David from King's School in Gloucester – for me. I barely dared pick up the receiver. He told me that he had rung, because there was one more important question that he needed to ask, which he had forgotten to put to me earlier in the day. At the same time, he was repeating how impressed he was, how well I came across etc etc. I tell you this, not to "boast", but because it seemed that he might be seriously thinking of offering me the job. The question he had overlooked earlier in the day, was "Would you be able to drive the School Minibus? It would be important for away fixtures, going to plays ….". As relieved as anything, I explained that I could not drive and therefore "Minibus duties" were impossible. He replied that therefore, that I would not be the right person. I graciously thanked him, we said our farewells and I put the phone down, a very relieved young man! I often wonder if I was only interviewed because of "David House" and that he felt sufficiently guilty to ring me and let me down "gently" by concocting a spurious reason why I was not the right candidate. I shall never know, but I suspect that we were both equally relieved to escape the situation, with our honour intact!

Anyway, I had another date to look forward to. This time, I took the train to Cheltenham on the Tuesday evening. I was to stay with Lesley and Derek, as Lesley had kindly offered to take me over the hill to Winchcombe for my interview and then collect me at the end of the day. The process was slightly different this time. I was one of six candidates to be interviewed on the same day. At the end of that day, the Head, the Governors and the Modern Languages Advisor for Gloucestershire would reach a decision and offer someone the job. Spoiler alert – you know the outcome! Yes, dear readers, I got the job. I was thrilled. Beyond thrilled. I was ecstatic! Lesley collected me, took me back to the station in Cheltenham and I was now a fully-fledged teacher!

I stayed at that school for five years, almost. I loved it. I loved the setting, nestling amongst the Cotswold Hills, I loved the children, I loved the trips we did, I loved the funny moments (of which there were many) and I loved being in the classroom.

But one day, after almost 5 years, another fortuitous and totally unplanned phone call altered the direction of my life entirely.

Three phone calls – Paris to Cheltenham, Cheltenham to Bristol and finally Winchcombe to London had a significant impact on the course of my career. The moral of the story therefore – don't phone anybody!

Painswick

29th May 2020

Dear Lucas and Charlotte,

It is great to learn from your Mum, that some activities are "returning to normal". It must be brilliant to be back horse-riding with Katherine, Charlotte and trips to the cycle scrambling track must be great fun, Lucas!

For us, nothing has changed. Iris still pops by to see us sometimes, on her way home. A few days ago, she brought us a present! Yes, sirree – our very own stick! Now, you will both remember the importance of a good stick – fundamental for any long walk, adventure in the park or for a trek to yon den. However, this was not just "any old stick". She had painted it, in rainbow colours and came down the steps to the patio, wielding it like a machine-gun. I begged her not to shoot us – and guess what – yup – play dead, Grandad!

Well not exactly true that nothing has changed – my hairdresser rang and has pencilled in an appointment for 8th July. I took the very first slot of the morning and have to wear a mask and gloves, so Boris permitting, I shall be back to normal that day! Also by then, Liverpool will have been crowned Premier League Champions. As games recommence on 17th June, and as we only need 3 more victories, the cup will be paraded through empty streets of Liverpool! Actually, it is an exciting prospect, to think that matches will resume and that sport will once again be a part of our lives. Hopefully, you'll both be back in training too, at some point in the not too distant future.

Kathy, Grandma's friend, came over from Cheltenham last Friday. She parked in the village car park and the two of them went for a walk around the village, home via the alpacas and coffee in the garden. Only the alpacas weren't there! Grandma was really disappointed, because she'd told Kathy all about them – and then they too had obviously gone for a walk – been taken out somewhere – in the opposite direction. Very kindly, Kathy brought some scones that she had made. I was allowed out too at this point, so we had "Cotswold Cream Tea" – very civilised!

On Wednesday evening, I was strategically positioned at the window in the lounge, overlooking the garden, eyes peeled on the night sky, towards the South West, where Tim Peake had assured me (on a radio clip from that morning) that I would be able to see Space X. He told me (and a few million others) that at 9.35, clear skies permitting, I would be able to see the International Space Station, followed by Space X at 9.50 pm. Conditions were perfect, it was a calm, clear evening, no cloud, no wind, a balmy night. I scoured the horizon, I watched the light fade gradually, I scanned the skyline near and far – to wit – nothing. I was dead disappointed, in myself, because I knew that I was looking in the right direction, at the right time, leaning out of the right window (Grandma was worried about me!) – but I couldn't glimpse any astronomical phenomena or passing rockets – at all. At 10 pm the News came on and informed me that launch had been aborted, due to bad weather! So, it wasn't me! I didn't miss seeing it, it just was not there to witness. What I don't know though, is when it is now due to take off.......one lovely aspect was the sight of bats darting across the garden, at about "window height". Just a few, but unmistakably bats – which I normally associate with later in the summer. I wouldn't have seen them, had I not been leaning out of t'window, so not a complete waste of 15 minutes!

Life in Lockdown

There is a cottage, next to a farm, up a lane nearby, which has now put jars of home-made honey outside, which you can buy - £3.50. We now just have to remember to take dosh with us, the next time we head off in that direction. We have already forgotten, at least twice, which is really annoying – but I don't think that they are going to run out – famous last words, Grandad!

I hope the stories are sufficiently surprising substitutes for poetry – I am working away at various sagas and situations, which I trust will make you smile. The story of Wayne still makes me chuckle, 45 years on, because my Dad was just sooooo horrified!

Just had your call Lucas – 95% in your French assessment – incroyable – super – excellent – well done toi!

Lots of love

Grandad x

Painswick

6th July 202

Dear Lucas and Charlotte,

Now that my creative juices are devoted to wordsearches, French lessons, video clips (a right little media industry!), my writing of stories has taken something of a backseat! However, finally, enclosed is part of the final story for this year!

I haven't heard, but assume that your three tropical fish: Trent, Alexander and Arnold have settled into their new home, Charlotte. Does the noise of the water heater keep you awake?! I wonder how difficult it was to "hoover the gravel" (I still don't get that!) or how straightforward an operation it is, to change/cleanse the water.

It now seems that come what may, you will both be back to school in September. It will have been 6 months away – wow! It will be very strange having to wear your uniform, pack your bags, remember all your belongings...every day!! In many respects I bet you can't wait.

The excitement for me, is that I shall be having a haircut on Wednesday morning. I must wear gloves and a mask, but at least I shall be back to my tidy self once more. I did flirt with the idea of keeping it "longer", but have decided that it is just toooo much trouble and as Grandma says, "it isn't a good look". She has an appointment for the following week.

I have sent away for a new pair of walking shoes. They should arrive in a few days' time. You saw the state of the ones I have been using for the past 3 months – and 700 miles – so it really was time to sort it out. I am 61 years old as you know, but my legs have suffered

Life in Lockdown | 119

premature ageing from this regime of daily treks – and they, my legs, are now actually 82! As I have recorded in my letters to you, we have witnessed burgeoning blooms, Spring emerge, plants grow, colours burst out and the seasons unfold, throughout the lockdown. So much time has elapsed that we are now beginning to witness the signs of decline....conkers are growing really quickly, the foliage is beginning to turn brown and flaky....sure indications that summer is in full swing and dare I say, beginning to turn towards the next season. I am not going to write the word, because that would just be...too much!

Grandad x

THE STORY OF HOTELS AND HOTEL DISASTERS

Rather unfairly, I have the reputation for being a little clumsy, nay accident-prone. Some might even go as far as to say that I'm a "walking disaster", an "accident waiting to happen" – (yes you, Grandma!). This is hugely over-exaggerated and unwarranted criticism. There is a grain of truth, in the sense that my lack of spatial awareness and poor balance does, very occasionally, lead to a small mishap, in the course of everyday situations. Most of these go unnoticed, unrecorded and "under the radar". It does seem to happen though, on a disproportionate number of occasions when I am staying in a hotel. Is it the unfamiliar surroundings, is it the bizarre layout of hotel rooms, is it the strange fixtures and fittings unique to every bathroom? I really don't know, but for some reason, accidents do befall me, when I am staying somewhere away from home. I wonder if that is why no one (apart from the Mother-in-Law – and she didn't escape unscathed…read on) will invite me into their home for a weekend away!

When I was working in international sales, a good proportion of my time was spent overseas. I was hugely privileged to visit some wonderful countries, beautiful cities and stay in very pleasant surroundings. I never took it for granted, as I checked into the Hilton, the Marriott or the "Inter-Conti", in some far-flung destination. Nearer to home, especially in Europe, I always tried to find a nice local hotel, privately owned, or "boutique-style", with a little atmosphere, individual furnishings and where I would be known and welcomed – as a person in my own right, rather than as another anonymous business traveller in a "chain". These "chains" can be very good, and are always very conveniently located for airports, city centre meetings (a must for work), so I have nothing against them. It is simply that a boutique establishment is usually much more friendly and intimate. If you can find a good one, it can make a huge difference, when you arrive in another city for another week of traipsing round the offices of book dealers, law offices or universities.

I was exceptionally lucky to find one such, in the 8th arrondissement of Paris. It was located in the rue des Saussaies, right opposite the Ministry of the Interior.

That building was of some historical significance, as it had served as Gestapo Headquarters during WW2. I digress. The location was perfect. All the international law firms, whom I needed to visit, were based in the immediate environs. The 8th and the 16th arrondissements are the preserve of the major French law firms. As with all 3* hotels in Paris, the rooms were not huge, but always comfortable. The welcome was always warm. The breakfast was always the same – as in all 3* establishments in the heart of the city – a bol of coffee, some tartines, a croissant, pain aux raisins or pain au chocolat – plus orange juice and a yoghurt. La serveuse, (as well as housekeeper) was Pierrette. Such was the frequency of my visits at one stage of my career, that she even knew my preferred flavour of yoghurt. She was charming, friendly and ever-attentive. It was a lovely start to each working day and a pleasure to return to the hotel, at the end of a busy day.

So much did I appreciate the hospitality, that when Carol and I decided to take her parents to Paris for a few days, the hotel was already decided! We were treated so kindly, and the fact that I had brought my family to stay at the hotel "got me millions of Brownie points" all round! Pierrette could not speak English. Therefore I did the translations for the breakfast orders – café au lait, café, thé – and so on. She then enquired about yoghurts. I explained the choices and Carol, Tony and Jean decided. "What about you?" asked Carol. "Oh Pierrette knows what I have", I replied. Not only that, she always brought me a pain aux raisins, if poss. She really did seem to "wait on me, hand and foot". As Jean remarked, with not a shred of irony or over-statement, "It's better treatment than he gets at home!". We all laughed, I had to translate for Pierrette, and she smiled shyly, laughed a little and said very kind things about me, and that it was a pleasure!

No dramas, no accidents, no mishaps there. Apart from Carol and her bag……

We went to Paris for the weekend, as we used to quite often – leave home early and be in the 8th for lunch – wonderful treat! On one occasion, in the cab from CdG airport – a white Peugeot – we chatted at length with the driver. He was Vietnamese. As we had been to that country, we talked in the fondest terms about his homeland – he reminisced about his childhood – and we were all very happy to have met and "shared a moment". He dropped us off, we checked in, went upstairs to our room, to dump our stuff quickly, before the obligatory "salade au chèvre chaud" and a large glass of red. (We always have that!). As we were about to leave, Carol said, "where's my handbag?". "Je ne sais pas", said I. When I realised she was serious, I reassured her that it would still be in Reception. It wasn't…..As the bag contained her credit cards and more importantly her passport, she was more than a little distressed. As you know, Grandma is enormously well organised, and therefore such occurrences are few, if ever! Being the Captain Sensible in this marriage, I asked the hotel to use their phone, to ring the Taxi Rank Office of "Groupe 7" at the airport, to make enquiries. I knew the driver was Vietnamese, I knew it was a white Peugeot, surely they would be able to identify the drop off in Rue des Saussaies and all would be well. During all of these explanations – good job I can speak French! – I caught a glimpse of a white car passing the front of the hotel. "A white Peugeot" I exclaimed, promptly ended the conversation and dashed out of the door. Sure enough it was THE cab, THE driver and he was getting out of the car, holding THE BAG! I shook his hand, thanked him profusely and thrust a generous tip into his hand – what a relief. By this point, Carol was also on the pavement, rushing towards the unsuspecting cab driver. She flung her arms round him, gave him a huge hug and uttered the immortal, multi-lingual words, "Merci, very much!". He beamed with delight, looking up at her smiling broadly – yes, he was that short – Grandma was taller than him – and was obviously delighted to "save the day". He saved the weekend too – passport, plastic and bag restored to Mrs. Parsons! So kind, so swift and so honest – what a wonderful guy. So you see, it is not just Grandad who has trouble in hotels!

That said, I discovered the Hotel des Saussaies on the recommendation of my friend Julian. I needed such advice because the previous "favourite" was now off-limits. This previous establishment, which shall remain nameless was in the "Marais" – the "Marshes". This is an old quarter of the city, that was as the name suggests, a less cultivated area of Paris, of old. Rue Vieux du Temple, ran the length of this "bohemian" corner, timber-framed buildings, very old, architecturally interesting structures line the street. Interspersed are several privately-owned 2* and 3* hotels

– the kind one finds all over the capital of France. I found one that I liked very much and stayed there regularly.

I used to spend many weeks a year visiting clients, but by Friday lunchtime was always eager to head back to the airport, for my "rush-hour" flight home. Appointments on Friday morning would end by noon, so that I could race back, check out, grab a cab and reach CdG for a 4 o'clock flight. Very often, I would cut it fine and was therefore was pressed for time. The very last time I stayed in this hotel, was just such an instance.

During my stay, the loo dripped and was quite an annoying sound. At night, even with the door closed, I could hear the constant "drip drip drip". I discovered though that if I removed the lid of the cistern and very gently removed the ballcock and had it wedged over the edge of the lip of said cistern, the dripping would cease. Every morning, very carefully, very tentatively, very "gingerly" and very cautiously, I would manoeuvre the metal bar back into the cistern and replace the lid. Job done. Cleaners would not see my handiwork, and all I had to do each night before bedtime was to repeat the procedure, to ensure a good night's sleep.

The day of departure – Friday – was going to be dead busy. As ever, I put the "Do not Disturb" sign on the door, to show that I was "still there". On return at noon, I would chuck my clothes in my bag, go to the loo and then check out – easy! Only, on this particular day, I had forgotten to ease the ballcock back inside the cistern….As I went to have a wee before leaving, as one always should "before leaving the house" or before going on a journey, I realised that the contraption was still resting, precariously, on the outside of the white porcelain container…In a panic, in a rush and certainly not taking sufficient care, I knocked down the seat and the plastic cover on the loo. This enabled me to climb up, to reach the ballcock, in order to carefully, tentatively, gingerly and cautiously, replace the bar and plastic ball, back where it belonged. Being in something of a hurry, I was rather less careful…I yanked the bar back, to enable me to ease it from under the lip of the cistern, but not knowing my own strength, ripped the bar off – totally. This was rather a shock, I lost my balance and went through the plastic loo seat cover, breaking it into two pieces, with my foot dangling over the bowl. Dear readers, I panicked. I had a bar, torn from the loo, two large jigsaw pieces of plastic loo and not very much time! I therefore did, what any right-minded person would. I chucked the bar and plastic ball inside the cistern, positioned the pieces of plastic on the seat, to cover the loo, picked up my bags, ran downstairs, checked out and "legged it", never to return. I suspect that there is still a warrant for my arrest circulating around the offices of the Parisian Tourist Police!

This little mishap was not, I must admit, not my first encounter with the vagaries of hotel accommodation. When I was working in the UK, I travelled all over the country and again, very often was required to be away from home. I therefore needed hotels, to stay in. I always used to wear a suit – very smart! Have you ever seen me in a suit? I suspect not – but that day will come, I'm sure. Anyway, when you're travelling all the time, sitting in a car, or in meetings, your trousers can become a little "crumpled". No? Well mine did! Again, Grandma was very keen that I always looked my best in "professional" situations. Unlike many men, I actually enjoy ironing. In fact, I would not let Grandma iron any of my shirts! I always had a clean one every day. I had a wide selection of ties, so that was good. At the end of each working day, I always had a pair of jeans and a casual (blue!) shirt to change into, for the evening. I would put my suit jacket on a hanger (to allow the creases across the back to fall out) and tried to make sure that the sleeves were not tooooo concertinaed around the elbow. That always happened to me, because I was writing notes or sitting with my hand under my chin, making a real mess of my sleeves. However, hanging it up as soon as possible each day, lessened the effect.

"What about your trousers Grandad"? I hear you ask. Ah well, thereby hangs a tale – but not a trouser press! "What is a trouser press, Grandad"? I hear you ask. Ah well, I shall enlighten you. As for creases on the jacket of a suit, the bottom half does not escape the rigours of a day sitting at the wheel of a car, or attending meetings. Creases behind the knees, over your tummy (if you have one, which I didn't in those days!), creases around your pockets ("never put your hands in your pockets, it looks messy and creates creases" said Grandma), as well as marks across the tops of your legs. The wear and tear on your ceks can be truly terrible. As I am not the tidiest guy in the world, Grandma always had to remind me of the need to take care of my appearance and to avoid any movement, or lack of, which could possibly result in my "looking a mess". She even bought me a crease-proof suit – travel friendly – that would go into a suitcase, that you could happily wear on a long-haul flight, that would be the perfect solution for the busy businessman. It might have been "crease proof", but unfortunately it was not "Grandad – proof"!

Trousers: very often in hotels, in those days, a "trouser press" would be provided in your room, especially those for business people. They could be self-standing. Imagine an ironing board on feet, that opens up, with a flap at the front. It is plugged in. You fold your trousers, as if to put them on a hanger. You then put them between the two elements – flap and "board", shut the flap, turn on the trouser press and leave said "hose" overnight. The warmth of the press, the pressure on the trouser legs means that knee creases are eliminated at the same time as maintaining a really sharp crease in the centre of the leg, thus making your trousers look as almost new as can possibly be achieved. A brilliant invention, which meant that every morning in a hotel, you could put on comfortingly warm, very smart trousers.

Self-standing trouser presses can take up a lot of space in the confined area of a hotel room. It is easy to knock them over, trip over the "feet" or to have to dodge around them. To prevent this, a practical solution was discovered. You could mount the entire thing on a wall. This would be at about waist height, to be as convenient as possible, it took little or no space and there would be no lead or wires across the floor – creating yet another hazard. Fitted to the wall, linked to the electricity socket, all you need do, is carefully, tentatively, gingerly and cautiously open the flap, fold your trousers, lay them delicately over the flap, shut said flap, flick the switch and let the machine do its job – perfect. In the morning you would simply open the flap, remove your beautifully restored legwear and head on down to breakfast. That is the theory, ladies and gentlemen.

I have explained that sometimes I was in a hurry. On one occasion, in Manchester, I had been a little late getting up. I jumped in the shower, dried myself, dressed quickly – shirt, tie, jacket and lastly therefore trousers and shoes. The trousers were in a wall-mounted press. I flicked the switch off – good boy. I opened flap – a little. I did not open it to its full extent. Instead I grabbed at my smart attire and pulled. This would allow me to take the trousers off the flap really quickly. I did not know my own strength. As I pulled, not very hard, or so I thought, not only did the trousers come, but the entire trouser press with them. I had tugged soooo hard that the entire device came away from the wall – oops.

I got dressed, leant the press against the wall, trying to mask the holes where the screws had come adrift – and said nothing. I don't think I have ever been to Manchester since – which is probably just as well!

Wall-mounted "things" can always be a hazard – in hotels, or at home. This element of the story is not strictly speaking the right place to be told, because it didn't happen in a hotel. That said, it wasn't actually my house either, so I suppose it does count. Several years ago, when Grandma and I were staying in Keswick, at Great Grandma's and Great Grandad's house, we were in the kitchen, waiting for your Mum and Dad to arrive. It was before you were born Charlotte – and Lucas was about 14 months old, so he won't remember what happened. Well, perhaps, deep down, he does retain a traumatic moment, that will remain with him all his days and may "resurface" as an "active memory" should a similar incident ever occur in his life!

You can see the kitchen and the table where we eat, in Keswick, can't you? On the wall, next to the window, you can imagine the cartoon picture of your Great Grandad hang-gliding – it's a gloriously funny and memorable image. Next to that is the "Officially Amazing" Certificate that Great Grandad received from the "Guiness Book of Records", when he became the oldest person to cycle from Land's End to John O'Groats – you know *exactly* where I mean, don't you? Well, I have to tell you that those items have not always been positioned on the wall, like that – no Sirree!

Before that, there was a set of wooden shelves, in pine, lovely, and on those shelves, Great Grandma had placed a full "dining service" – plates, cups, saucers, dishes – beautifully displayed. They were a focal point, and complemented all the ornaments and dishes on the large "Welsh Dresser" behind Great Grandma's chair. I always sit opposite the window, as you know – I always have, always will. There is absolutely no reason, no need, for me to go around, to the other side of the dining table. However, for some reason, on this fateful day, I was by the window. Perhaps I had been looking for a biro, next to the phone – I can't remember. What I do remember though, as does everyone who witnessed the following events (including possibly Lukey, but we don't know if this long-buried trauma will emerge one day), is that as I went around the table, inexplicably, I just did not see the shelves with the beautiful dinner service delicately placed upon them.

At that moment, Jason came through the kitchen door, holding you Lucas, in his arms. You were grizzly, mewling and not in any mood to be consoled. You had been unceremoniously woken up, from a lovely sleep in the back of the car, during the journey from York. Whenever you were awoken in such circumstances, as a toddler, you just did not like it, you did not appreciate being disturbed in your wonderful, infantile slumbers – and didn't we know it. The noise was incessant, Bless! I was so pleased to see you and Daddy, that I rushed by the table – seeing both of you – not the shelves. I bumped into them. No I banged into them. No, I clattered into them. No, I went headlong into them. I sent the whole thing flying. I smashed everything. Every cup, every saucer, every plate and every dish crashed to the floor, with an enormous smattering sound as each item of the dinner service smashed into smithereens on the tiled floor of the kitchen. Now, that did have the desired effect Lucas! You immediately stopped whinging and whining, your little face in rapt silence as you witnessed your very own clown performance from the circus. Not a sound, as you witnessed the scene of dinner service devastation before your eyes. No one said a word. Everyone looked on, in horror, but we all noticed that you were shocked into silence, Lucas!

Great Grandma was the first to speak. Very kindly, very quickly and very reassuringly, she said, "oh, it doesn't matter John, don't worry love, I never really liked that dinner service anyway". She was very understanding, and even if she didn't mean it, she was swift to say nice things and say, "it was an accident, these things happen", before fetching a dustpan and brush, to begin clearing the mess, strewn far and wide across the entire surface of the kitchen floor. Your Grandma was somewhat less understanding, she was very annoyed with me for being so clumsy. To this day, you might have noticed that whenever we visit the Gift Shop of a Stately Home or of a Castle she always makes me wait outside, or to take off my rucksack before I enter, and to make sure that I take care walking around. Now you know why! She always surveys the shop layout, casts an eye over potential areas of danger and alerts me to those – just in case! You know the expression, "like a bull in a china shop" – our family version of that is, "like Grandad in a …..shop" - no, just – "like Grandad".

The next hotel story most definitely was NOT my fault. I was not in the wrong, I didn't break anything and I was totally justified in asking the Manager for a refund. Read on….

I was spending a week in Zurich. It is a city which I like, I enjoyed working there and over a number of years had got to know my clients very well. Some, had become good friends. One evening, when I returned to my hotel, there was a group of Chelsea fans on the terrace outside, enjoying a beer. They were wearing the blue Chelsea strip and I realised that they were in Switzerland for a mid-week European match – playing "Grasshoppers", I think. As I passed by, I said, "Good Luck tonight, guys". Even though I am a Liverpool fan, it would have been churlish not to wish an English team success on a European night of football. They realised – obviously – that I was English and invited me to join them for a drink. I did. We chatted about the match, their chances, the journey, their impressions of Zurich. I told them that I was there "on business" and would not be at the game, but assured them that I would find a bar, where I could watch "Chelsea win". After that, I went back to my room, changed into my jeans and (blue!) shirt, before writing up my notes from that day. I then walked through the city centre to find somewhere for dinner and then to watch Chelsea. I have no recollection as to who won, what the score was and whether it was a good game, or not. The events of the rest of that night have obliterated the memory of a mere game of footie!

At the end of the evening, I returned to my hotel, took the lift up to the 3rd floor and went back to my room. I rang Grandma, as I always did before going to bed, I watched the late news on TV and then snuggled down for a good night's sleep. Or so I thought……..

At some point in the middle of the night (it turned out that it was 3.15), I was suddenly awoken by a really loud bang. I sat up, startled into immediate wakefulness, and saw a blue clad Chelsea fan coming into MY bedroom. It was not HIS bedroom. Bizarrely, I remember he was also wearing a Chelsea cap. Rather than say, " I'm awfully sorry old chap, but I think you're in the wrong room" – I jumped out of bed, shouting at him to get out, I raced across the room and chased him down the corridor, still shouting. He understood that 314 was not HIS bedroom! Because I had shouted so loudly, inevitably and unfortunately, I had disturbed other guests in the hotel. Next door to me, a little old lady had opened her door and peered along the corridor, wondering what on earth the commotion was at 3.15 in the morning. I walked back towards my room, being watched by this curious old dear. It was at this point, I remembered that I had just jumped out of bed, in the middle of the night and was not wearing my jim-jams (never took them on work trips), nor was I wearing the complimentary bath robe, nor was I wearing my knicks – in fact I was stark naked. Ooops! I'm not sure whether she was more shocked by the disturbance, or the sight of a middle-aged man walking nude towards her. I said, "Good night – he came into the wrong room", as I shut my door behind me!

Next morning, I remonstrated with the Manager, who was reluctant to offer me a refund, or to offer any logical explanation as to how a Chelsea fan had entered my room! During that day, I had a series of meetings with international law firms around the city. In one of those meetings, with a client whom I knew really well, I related the story of the events from the night before. He laughed. He thought it highly amusing (by this time I was "milking it" and telling the story against myself). My indignation at the seemingly thoughtless response from the Manager of the hotel had not diminished – in fact if anything, it had increased! My lawyer friend, through tears of mirth, offered to write a legal complaint on my behalf. He WAS serious, even though he thought everything was dead funny. I WAS tempted, but common-sense kicked in. I told him that it wasn't that much of a big deal and that the old lady was probably still in a state of shock, and that it was her who really should be submitting an official complaint – for having to witness a naked Englishman running down the corridor "in the wee small hours"! Suffice it to say, when I did leave on the Friday afternoon, the cost for one night's accommodation was deducted from my bill. And that is why nowadays I do always wear my jim-jams – and don't support Chelsea!!

Vienna is a beautiful city. The architecture is stunning, the cobbled streets full of atmosphere and it is somewhere that holds a very special place in my memories. The very first time I visited, having arrived late on the Sunday evening, the entire city was blanketed in a covering of snow. By the Monday morning, as I opened my curtains, looking out onto St. Stephen's Cathedral, the sky was gun grey, there was not a sound and the snow was so thick that there was no movement whatsoever in the streets below. It is an image that will remain with me, always. It became evident that all of Vienna was at a standstill. I tried to make some phone calls, to find out if I would be able to walk across the city centre for a series of meetings. Nobody answered – there was nothing to be done, other to venture out into the snow-sodden streets and to enjoy the privilege of seeing Vienna as a trapped "tourist". It was truly magical. The horse-drawn carriages were lined up outside the Hofburg Palace, all looking very sorry for themselves, no one going anywhere. Snow was falling, from a leaden sky as I trudged through the city centre, transfixed by the sheer beauty of the buildings, enhanced by the covering of snow. It brought to mind the very first phrase I learnt in German. To be more accurate, the very first expression in German, that my Dad taught me. "mit Schnee bedeckt" – blanketed in snow. I remember it still, and now the words evoke not just memories of my Father, but also of one of the most glorious moments, when Vienna truly was "blanketed in snow".

That, by way of introduction, can now be besmirched by another, less glorious moment, in this wonderful city. As ever, I was there on a business trip. You know the routine by now. I was in a very nice hotel, convenient for meetings – all the International Law Firms were housed in beautiful buildings around the "Ring". It quite literally is a "ring road" which encircles the historic heart of Vienna. A tram runs around the entire circle – and it almost is – a proper circle – you can hop on and hop off, dead easy, dead cheap (or was in those days), and it was the city in which I created my record of "most meetings in one day" – 11 to be precise, aided by their proximity to each other – either on foot, or by use of said tram!

Notwithstanding this fact, on the last day, as ever, I was in a rush, once I returned to my hotel, to check out and then jump in a cab to the airport. I had a large, hard suitcase in those days. Naturally it had a pull-up handle, so that it could be wheeled through the concourse of railway stations, or across the departure hall in an airport. As I came down in the lift, my computer bag was resting on top of the suitcase, shoulder strap in my hand around the pull-up handle of the case. The lift reached the ground floor, the doors of the lift opened, I tilted the case and moved forward – quickly – to exit towards Reception. I went through the open doors – but at that point ground to a halt. The large case would not fit through the aperture. Now, at this stage, I have been told, what I should have done, was to stop, turn the case sideways through 90 degrees and then leave the lift. My spatial awareness is nil, at the best of times. On this occasion I was in a hurry, so such simple logic eluded me. I decided that the best solution was to exert a little more pressure – to pull a little harder. So that's what I did. In fact I gave it such an enormous yank that indeed it did come through – hoorah! No – not exactly. As the large, heavy suitcase came through the doors of the lift, it caught the edge of the surround, the façade of the exterior of the lift. This was a large, colourful surround, depicting an idyllic countryside scene from the Austrian Tyrol. The image was designed to show the beauty of the Austrian mountains (think "Sound of Music"-esque). The suitcase did not in fact just clip the edge of this "stage-scenery" – no, I pulled so hard that it came away from the lift – in a single piece – both sides and the top and dropped around me, to the floor, with a crash. It wasn't broken, had simply come way from its "moorings". I looked at it, slightly taken aback, because even by my standards, this was a bit extreme, stepped over it, approached Reception, apologised profusely, checked out and ran! Suffice it to say, I never returned!

I spent about 10 weeks every year in Germany. By the simple law of averages, something was bound to go wrong, at some point. You need not be disappointed, dear readers. This saga unfolded in Frankfurt, but it could quite easily have been any city. I was staying on the 6th floor of a "chain" hotel, I forget which. When I'm away on business, especially in Europe, I tend not to be concerned about "security", and therefore don't lock doors at night, simply shut them. For some inexplicable reason, one day in this particular hotel, I slid the chain across the door. Why – I have no idea! However, when I tried to slip the chain backwards, to allow me to open the door, I discovered that I could not. It was one of those bizarre contraptions that requires you to use both hands. One to slide the chain, the other to hold back a little "latch", to allow it to slide. Try as I might, I just could not manage this simple task – for reasons I need not clarify! I was trapped!

I therefore rang Reception, to explain my dilemma. I asked for someone to come and "release" me. I had some difficulty explaining exactly how and why I was potentially entombed in their establishment. The "I can't use both hands" was easy to say. It was however, impossible to convey the fact that holding both elements, simultaneously, was physically beyond me. The Receptionist gave up, but kindly said that she would someone "up". I waited. I anticipated a knock on the door at any moment. Nothing happened, No one came. Then, I heard "tap tap tap" on the window. I turned round, to see a guy, in blue overalls, standing in a "cage" – not totally enclosed – but like a huge metal basket, normally the preserve of window cleaners. What he, and then I, realised, was that although he had kindly managed to reach the 6th floor – there was no way into the room, from outside. All air-conditioned rooms, therefore no need to be able to open the window and as a safety measure too, in order to prevent people falling, or jumping….from a great height, onto the paving stones below. He smiled, he shrugged and then he disappeared. "That's it", I thought. "I'm trapped, there's no way out!".

A few minutes later though, there was a knock on the door, and a voice, in German, (after all this was in Frankfurt!) said, "Hello, Sir. Please stand back from the door". I did as I was told. Next thing, like a scene from a TV show, the blue overalls appeared….the "odd-job" man had shoulder-barged through the door! The chain, the lock, the entire mechanism flew through the air. The gentleman came to a halt, half way across the room, and said, "Guten Tag, Herr Parsons". He then picked up the debris of what had been the chain, the lock, as well as the screws holding it in the wall. Without another word, he went into the "Bob the Builder-style" belt, around his waist, took out a screwdriver, took all the pieces and screwed everything back into place, checked it worked, picked up the splinters of wood around the door, said, "Alles Gut – Auf Wiedersehen", smiled and left. No fuss, no telling off, no dramas – it was as if he was simply checking whether I wanted Room Service! What a wonderful man! Suffice it to say, I have NEVER, EVER, shut and locked a hotel with the chain since that day!

Grandma has mostly escaped witnessing my misadventures in hotels. I always admit to my mistakes, as we all know, "honesty is the best policy", so I never hide from the disasters I have created. Hearing about such mishaps, "after the event" and not having been directly involved, she has invariably seen the funny side, and often, she even tells these stories to her friends. "You'll never guess what John has done now", before regaling everyone with tales of the scenes of devastation, I have left in my wake, around the world. It was always "funny" because she was not involved……well, until one rather dramatic incident in Kunming.

"Where is Kunming, Grandad?" – "Ah well, long story short, it is in North Western China. I had a bit of an incident there. Nuff said"! "No it isn't Grandad…what happened, exactly?". Ah, yes. Kunming. The start of a really adventurous holiday.

We were travelling to the Tibetan plateau for a summer holiday. We were looking forward to beautiful scenery, Shangri-La, mountains, culture, glorious food – but it is quite a complicated journey. We had arrived in Kunming very late one night, before a very early start for a morning flight from Kunming, up to the plateau. It was a small, very modest, not very modern hotel in the city. We arrived some time after 11 pm and as we needed to leave again at 5 am, we went straight to bed, as we had been travelling for a very long time and we were both dead tired. Before jumping into bed, we both had a wee and brushed our teeth. As I shut the bathroom door behind me, it scraped across the tiled floor and made an awful screeching noise – rather like chalk on a blackboard, the sound of which really grates and seems really loud. I made a mental note to try and avoid that scraping early next day, before we left, as everyone else would be fast asleep. Nothing, if not considerate and aware of others….

The alarm was set and allowed me time for a swift shower. Wherever I am, whatever the time or indeed the circumstances, I always like to freshen up by jumping under a jet of hot water, however briefly. This occasion was no exception and I thought that the rush of water would wake me up too, as we had only had a few hours' sleep. Enough for Grandma, but certainly not for moi.

In my semi-conscious state, I said, "I'll go to the bathroom first". I dodged the bed, the cases and opened the bathroom door. It scraped a little. Mindful of not wanting to disturb our neighbours, as I entered the bathroom, I decided that I should shut the door, but try to prevent any more grating, scraping sounds. (I was not wearing my jim-jams – don't take them on holiday, unnecessary space and weight in my suitcase).

I am quite strong. My left arm has always done all the work: lifting, driving, writing, everything. The early morning, half asleep logic told me that if I lifted the door, ever-so-gently, and pulled it shut at the same time, it would avoid the awful screechy sound. I did! However, I did not realise my own strength. As I lifted the door, it turned out to be with rather more force than I had anticipated. It wasn't a gentle movement at all. In fact, I think it is fair to say that I under-estimated my power, because as I lifted, the entire door came away in my hand – yes, just the left hand – as ever..

Three tiny hinges had popped out, such had been the force I exerted on the door. "Oh dearie me", said I. Those might not have been my *exact* words! I am now wide-awake, stark naked, at 4 am, with a bathroom door in my hand.

"What have you done now?" hissed Grandma from the bedroom. The "now" suggests that this is not the first occasion on which she has asked about my actions.

Thinking really quickly by this stage – my brain is working full tilt now, I said "In 5 years' time, you'll really see the funny side of this – honestly – can we therefore fast-forward 5 years and laugh NOW?". I suspected that I knew what Grandma's response would be – I was not wrong. Fast-forwarding 5 minutes was rather more of a priority. I think that it is fairly safe to say, at that point, that Grandma was not amused and didn't appreciate the surreal humour of the image she was about to behold – her darling husband, in his Birthday suit, holding a door, in the middle of the night, in a modest Chinese hotel in Kunming.

Realising that DIY is not my forté, Grandma's main concern was to repair the damage that I had, so considerately and yet so disastrously wrought upon this room. She suggested that I get in the shower. I insisted otherwise. As she isn't that tall, or indeed that strong (when it comes to manoeuvring full-size doors), I explained that I could "help". Now, I know that probably didn't sound toooo convincing, at that moment, but I am taller – and stronger – evidenced by my taking the door off its hinges in the first place! Between us, we managed to attach the very top hinge back into the bracket. Try as we might, and with not a huge amount of time available, we had to abandon our endeavours. Therefore the door was left flapping, and actually, not scraping AT ALL! I did jump in the shower, we packed – and ran! Fortunately the return leg of our journey, at the end of the trip, did not require an overnight stop in Kunming!

Disasters, accidents, mishaps happen to everyone. I just seem to have more than my fair share! However, it isn't always the case.

If I may, allow me to take you back to Vienna. On a trip there, a couple of years after wrecking the surround of the lift, a lawyer friend recommended that I stay in a brand new hotel, on the "Ring". It had "opening week" offers and deals, it was part of "Le Meridien", a very good standard, so I decided to stay there, It was very good, the staff were attentive and it was clearly obvious that everyone was trying really hard to make a fantastic impression, given it was the vey first week that they had been open. It was really convenient for all my meetings, so it all went very well. There were a few "teething troubles", nothing major, nothing to complain about and nothing to about which to be concerned. When I checked out on the Friday (no, I didn't break anything, no I didn't destroy the lift), the Receptionist asked – as they always do – if everything had been fine during my stay. I said that it was all good, but may I please have a word with the Manager. This seemed to be a "contradiction in terms" – "fine" "but can I speak to the Manager?". She looked quite concerned and I reassured her, that I was not about to complain!

The Manager, once summoned, came from the office straight away. I congratulated him on the hotel, the staff, in their very first week. I added, cautiously, a few comments, emphasising that I was not complaining, I didn't want a refund, I wasn't being a pain, it was simply to highlight a couple of things, which he may not be aware of. I don't even remember what I said, but the comments must have been about the smooth running of the place. He thanked me, wished me safe journey and said that they at the hotel looked forward to seeing me again, "next time". I went to the airport – all well.

About a week later, I received a letter at home. It was from the Manager of Le Meridien Vienna. He thanked me for my "feedback" and as a gesture of appreciation, offered me a complimentary weekend break at the hotel, for 2 people! What a lovely, kind, totally unexpected gesture. As Grandma had never been, it would be a great opportunity to visit Vienna as "tourists". Le Meridien, ideally located on the "Ring" was perfect for a leisure visit, just as well as business.

I found convenient dates, I managed to book flights using Air Miles and so we set off, in the October of that year for a weekend in Vienna, which was not costing us a penny! The flight arrived safely and we were in the hotel by lunchtime. Although I knew that we couldn't check in, I wanted to drop off our bags, before walking into the centre for lunch. At Reception, they greeted us warmly and said, "Unfortunately your suite isn't ready yet, Mr. and Mrs. Parsons". "No problem, may we just leave our bags with you until later?" said I. We walked out, I led the way because I had chosen the venue in advance and once outside, said to Grandma, "Don't get your hopes up. This is a "freebie", it won't ACTUALLY be a suite". We agreed that the Receptionist had just used the English word "suite" by mistake.

Later in the afternoon, we returned, we checked in and we were led up to our room. Dear readers, it WAS a suite. It was a HUGE suite, on the corner of the hotel, so we had glorious views in 23 directions. We had a bedroom, a sitting room, walk in wardrobes and the most lovely furniture. What a lovely surprise!

Painswick

13th July 2020

Dear Lucas and Charlotte,

Enclosed a poem, for which the inspiration came from the exploits of a certain football manager! You will be glad to know that I have sent a copy to him, in the post, at Anfield. Do you also remember that some time ago, he wrote to a little boy (a Manchester United fan) who asked that he have his team lose a few games "to give others, i.e. Man U a chance"? It received huge press coverage, because of the response he sent.

Juergen replied, congratulating the child on his passion for HIS team, but also explained that the respect for each other's success was an important dimension to competitiveness in sport. I thought that was wonderful. I don't expect a reply for one second, but hope at the very least, that he does actually see it. No doubt there is a team of "office-bods" who deal with all the correspondence, (of which there will be HUGE volumes), and I'm sure he sees very little of what "he" receives.

The last week of "school" for another year. Wow, how weird has this one been? In previous years, the passage of time, for me in many respects, has been marked by Easter Hols, half term, Summer – never mind Birthdays or New Year. Seeing both of you as the school calendar trundled by, seemed to give a pattern to the seasons even. Not so, 2020!

That said, it was lovely to be with you in York a few weeks ago and we are now both really excited at the prospect of your visit next week.

Life in Lockdown | 139

Grandma has gone out to have her hair done (especially!) today – the first time in several months! She can't wait to look her "old self" again. Am I "allowed" to say old self, when talking about a lady who is soon to be 68 years old?!!

I received my new shoes this morning. They are dead smart, a comfy fit and should enable me to hit the hills again – for yet another 1,300 miles!

Lots of love,

Grandad x

ODE TO JUERGEN (7/7/20)

The thirty years of hurt have gone
As now the Premiership is won
When the 19-20 season came to a stop
You really had to feel for Juergen Klopp.
Covid caused all games - to be put on hold
The trophy from us was almost "stole"
When dey said, "we'll cancel this campaign"
Who knew if the chance would come again
To lead the pack – more than twenty points ahead
I can't imagine what words at Anfield could have been said….
The possibility that this campaign would be null and void
An outcome that at all costs, we needed to avoid
It was though, really, a poss-ib-il-ity
An incomprehensible outcome, that would've been for me.

But no, the crown is ours, the trophy won
The work on the pitch though, is not yet done.
We've got records we need to chase
And games to win – that's just in case
Anyone dares suggest we've lost the plot
Not a chance – it's just comments from a churlish lot
Of other fans, who don't appreciate
That LFC can be this great……..
The team, the squad have been sublime
All stars, all heroes, they will stand the test of time!
Trent with the beloved sixty six
Bamboozles opponents with his "assists"
The crosses inch perfect into the box
The ball at the striker's feet it drops

Life in Lockdown | 141

And then, one can say, more often than not
The goalie's beaten with a glorious shot!
Whether Salah, Mane or Fab-in-ho
We're pretty certain – no we deffo know
The ball is struck - is goalward bound.
And as it hits – a unique sound
The KOP – it roars, it sings, it cheers
That blessed sound to those who hear
The celebrations – the undiluted glee!
The flags they wave, for all to see
Our unique fans, chant in appreciation
The most passionate lot, of the entire nation!
They love the journey, love the play
And love it when they hear Klopp say
"Success is good, of course we want to win
But that is NOT the only thing
We must play well, always try our best
If that's the case, we know the rest
Our fans are with us, they warrant what they deserve
And now it's happened – after thirty years"!
There's only one thing that's left to say
The Anthem we know as - Y.N.W.A.

AFTERWORD

It is now the end of July 2020. At the beginning of this month, lockdown restrictions were eased. People have been encouraged to return to work where possible and practical, albeit with the precaution of face-masks and continued social distancing. Pubs and restaurants have re-opened, with a degree of caution as well as optimism that business can be generated and a return to some sort of normality, especially during the summer holidays. Families have been able to meet; we are no exception.

**"July 22nd 2020 - Grandma's Birthday —
such a happy day to be reunited at last!"**

Last week, to celebrate Carol's Birthday, Lucas and Charlotte with their parents, came to stay with us for 48 hours. The weather was kind, the reunion was wonderful and for two days we did everything we always do, when the children come and visit during the School summer holidays.

We played boules in the garden, we went to the park where we enjoyed table-tennis, frisbee and a family game of cricket. The revelation was that Charlotte has also started to play and is an accomplished bowler – how brilliant!

The following day we went to the woods, to check on our den. A few running repairs, before we headed across country to Edge. I had booked a table on the terrace of the Edgemoor Inn. A celebratory Birthday lunch for Grandma – finished off with a huge Sundae for Lucas and Charlotte – because that is what they always have! A leisurely walk back to Dover Cottage, across the fields and then Birthday Cake and fizz on the patio – a glorious day, a lovely celebration and the belief that perhaps, just perhaps, we are now leaving coronavirus behind.

Dover Cottage
July 31st 2020